Questions
BEFORE COMMITMENT

Andrew Balkcom and Ashleigh Maldonado

authorHOUSE®

AuthorHouse™
1663 Liberty Drive
Bloomington, IN 47403
www.authorhouse.com
Phone: 1-800-839-8640

Published by AuthorHouse 3/28/2013

ISBN: 978-1-4817-2164-6 (sc)
ISBN: 978-1-4817-2163-9 (e)

Library of Congress Control Number: 2013903793

Book Design by: Sonia Fiore and Andrew Balkcom

Any people depicted in stock imagery provided by Thinkstock are models, and such images are being used for illustrative purposes only. Certain stock imagery © Thinkstock.

This book is printed on acid-free paper.

Acknowledgments

Ashleigh Maldonado

I wish to express my deepest appreciation to several people for helping me realize my dream of bringing this book to the reading public.

First and foremost, I would like to thank Andrew Balkcom for trusting me with his ideas for this book and for allowing me to express my life experiences. This exemplifies the essence of a great friend.

To my son, Stefan—I am doing all this to provide a better life and a secure future for you. To his father, Edwin Pratt—I can't thank you enough for being a great father and supporter of our child.

To my daughters, Jazmyn and Salena—my lovely baby girls are the reason I smile every day with wonder and amazement. My joy and love expands without limits because you two continue to teach me how to be a better parent.

To my parents, Jose and Anna Maldonado—I want to thank you for raising me, pushing me through high school and giving me the opportunity to attend college. I absolutely appreciate all the continued support. May you forever rest in peace.

To all of my family—I am forever grateful for your support!

To my closest friends, for at some point in my journey, all of you have helped and supported me: Timothy Hampton, Valerie and Mark Scharff, LaToya Montgomery, Jenilyn Villamor, April Thompson, Darrell Pollard, Kathy Lee, Kourbine Lee, Carly Turner, Kimberly Dixon, Acheri Donnell, Deborah Porter-Stringer, Donna Miller, Dawn Hallman, Charlotte Rose, Lora Garner, Tamontae Jenkins, John Barge, Jermaine Evans, Darnell Thompson, Demondrey White, Pastor James Cunningham, Derrick Thompson, Antone Murray, Sal Preciado, LaKeisha Hunter, Sonia Fiore, Kristen Bensch, and anyone I may have forgotten. *Thank you!*

Andrew Balkcom

I would also like to dedicate this book to my father Andrew Hall aka "West Side Slim." I would like to express my deepest gratitude to all my family and friends for helping my dreams come true. First to Ashleigh Maldonado for taking time out of her busy schedule to put these ideas on paper to create such a helpful book.

To my daughters, LayLay and Sydney, this is dedicated to you when you get older and are able to experience the joy of love don't forget to ask a lot of these questions before you get committed. I Love you all so much. To Peggy Taylor, here is to us because if we would have asked these important questions then--maybe our relationship would have gone into a different direction.

To my beautiful mother Patricia Balkcom, Brothers John, William, and Alexander, Sister Amber, aunts and uncles, and loving Grandma. To my Stepmother Denise Drain, her Sister Patricia and family.

To Candace Eason and her family, I thank you so much for loving me for who I am and putting up with my crap. Crystal McKinney, I thank you so much for sticking by me after my father's death and allowing me to stay with you and your beautiful kids Trent and Juliana. I will always love you guys.

To my closest friends, thanks-at some point all of you have helped and supported me: David Lawrence, Christ Meza, Dwyane Wade Sr., Beverly Kee, Lilie Love, Tomeka Napper, Mark Dubuclet and Ron Boyd, K Joy, Chad Carpenter, Auntie Karen and Nicole Jackson, Dr. Ahmad Glover, DJ Billy Rice, Angie B, Eli Mualin, Christopher White, Tony Major, Fabian, Arleen and Juan Betancourt, Michael Ficarra, Alejandro Rubinstein, Sam Robinson, Gerald Celestin, Jourdan Saunders, Jennifer, Jose Perez, Roberto Kasinsky, Tricia Drummond, John Nittolo, Nadar, Darrel Cox, Ivan Weavers, Lekan Salaam, Ali, Kevin Harper, Tony Blades, Jacky Hamlin, Ms. Loretta, Larry Dozier, Rev. Clark, Cristina Thompson, Sandy and family, James Smith, Pastor Johnson and family, Kenny Long, April, David Boyden, and whomever I did not mention, it was not on purpose. I thank you.

Introduction

Almost everyone enters into a relationship in the honeymoon stage of dating. It is fun at first—the physical attraction, the cute first moments, and the dating adventures. This beginning is called the "meeting of the two representatives." When the two meet, they are meeting each other's representative or the person they would like the other to "think" they really are. And so, at first, it would seem as if the two of them have very much in common.

There may be many signs of discord among couples, but these signs are often overlooked by the animalistic attraction or the need to find that "special soul mate." Later, as the relationship progresses, the couple realizes that they were not suited for one another.

Couples split because of different beliefs, cultural or family conflicts, but they mainly split because of a lack of communication before entering the relationship. They ask many menial questions such as, "What is your favorite color, food, television show or movie?" These questions have no bearing on how your relationship is going to function.

Later, after the break-up, the only communication is arguing over who bought the items the couple acquired in the household while they lived together and who gets to keep or sell them. This boils down to a waste of time and a painful, sometimes costly learning experience.

In order to experience pain from a broken heart, you have to know love. Love and hate are on the same spectrum, but they are on opposite sides of the scale. Still, you have to keep the balance, even when it feels as if your emotions are all mixed up and spinning out of control. No one intentionally places him- or herself in a position to be hurt by someone, but love or lust will have a person make some odd decisions.

We guarantee that anyone who reads this book will relate in some way to what this book has to offer. Simply asking some of the questions suggested in this book will help you gain insight into your other half. Whether you are using these questions as icebreakers or just as some playful quizzing between partners, you will realize you failed to ask some important questions before you committed.

My question to you is, are you ready to better prepare yourself before entering into a relationship, friendship, engagement, or marriage?

Question 1
Are You Single?

Rightfully, this should always be the first dating question before even asking someone's name. If the person is attached, married or has a significant other, there shouldn't be a need to ask any further questions.

Ashleigh: Men feel that women always wait for a man to approach them. There's a perceived notion that it is easy to read the signs from across the room and make one's way over to speak—only to be rejected.

Andrew: Women hardly ever feel it necessary to approach men, nor do they feel comfortable doing so. But if a woman does, she gets straight to the point about her purpose or reason for wanting to meet him.

Are you single? For some people, this question has many different meanings, when it really has only one, suitable for one person only. When you approach someone and ask this question, and the person replies, "No, I am married," the advance should stop there. The idea is to refrain from asking pointless questions that are not conducive to continuing the conversation. A question such as, "Are you happily married?" can be interpreted as blatantly disrespectful and rude. An approach in that vein is a back door to an opportunity in the conversation to elicit privileged information for continued discussion. Remember that the back door option of finding out problematic issues in other people's relationships reveals a weak premise and should be dismissed. Conventional wisdom states that if a person is in a relationship, no matter whether he or she is married, unhappily married, or on the verge of a break-up, the person is still not single! Upstanding women generally are more suited to originality. It would be nice to hear, "I am interested in you ... I may not be your type, but I still would like to know if you are single." If not, "It was a pleasure to meet you."

Respect and integrity in relationships and marriages has seemingly decreased over the years. Why? It could be that women are not used to being approached correctly. When the approach shows no regard to caution, unheeded persistence can be annoying and create snobbish attitudes. Despite the dating atmosphere, certain rules and mannerisms should be observed, and both women and men should be cordial and respectful of each other's feelings.

Question 2

What is His/Her Sexual Orientation?
Straight, Gay, Lesbian, or Bisexual?

Ashleigh: Men tend to have women believe that they would like to watch a threesome or that a woman can be intimate with another female if he is around. It's intriguing to them. Men feel that women can't fulfill what they can do—even with a strap-on dildo.

Andrew: For most women it is *not* okay if their partners engage in sexual acts with others and still maintain autonomy with them at the same time. Some women may be possessive, jealous, insecure, and may only go so far as to what they will share with someone else in the bedroom.

A young lady is leaving a bar and is approached by a married couple. Without any semblance of protocol, the couple stops to ask the young lady whether she is gay or straight and whether she would go home with them. There was no question as to whether she was attached or otherwise, no question as to her name, and no question as to whether she goes both ways. Needless to say, the young lady was rather shocked, wondering if this approach was status quo these days. She said no and walked away quickly. This scenario is a good lesson. You should *not* to take what you see on the surface as the final assessment without going deeper, but you should know how to approach a woman and what to say.

Bottom line, you have to know whether the question you ask is appropriate. When meeting a person for the first time, the signs, be they real or imagined, are not that easy to read anymore! The stereotypical gay man does not wear a "flaming" wardrobe with a sassy sweet attitude to match. Let's not forget the "undercover brother," the man who has been married to a woman for years who may have a man on the side.

Question 3
Are You an Honest Person?

◇◇◇◇◇◇◇◇◇◇◇◇◇◇◇◇◇◇◇◇◇◇◇◇◇◇◇◇◇◇◇◇◇◇◇◇◇◇◇

Ashleigh: Men tell women what they think they want to hear, what they think would please them, and what they think they can get away with in a given situation. Furthermore, men are likely to minimize dialogue as to not incriminate themselves with things to remember or lies to keep straight. Less is better.

Andrew: Women are nurturers and geniuses in the art of deceit —they effectively use guile and coyness to keep men off-balance when they are in control. Masking techniques are in place, and they play the all-assuming role of family matriarch to stay in control. That's why kids never know that mom is struggling or in pain—she masks it well. They often give too much information and detail in any given situation to make it difficult for men to recite back, if necessary.

This is a question that I am sure is rarely asked before entering into a relationship, but a person's honesty should be ascertained early, before any commitment is rendered. The answer should be yes or no, without any degrees of compromise—no gray areas. Being totally honest is telling the truth. Avoiding the truth, non-disclosure, or telling a story to show you in a favorable light is not being honest. Asking that question is a good litmus test to gauge how one would answer.

Question 4
Does He/She Open the
Car Doors for You?

If your answer is *no,* but you like to have the door opened for you, ask him to do so.

Ashleigh: Men do things like this when they feel it is appropriate, not necessarily when a woman feels it should happen.

Andrew: Women like spontaneity; don't only be spontaneous when you are going out somewhere fancy.

Chivalry is not dead. Men, forever be gentlemen. When you are going out somewhere, let her know you appreciate her company and open doors for her. Women, if he does not behave like anything resembling a gentleman, don't assume that he has no manners or that he is not for you. He may not have been raised in a godly way, where home training and manners were part of molding a man.

Imagine you're on a date with a girl, and she happens to behave as if she expects you to be the perfect gentleman. You park in front of a restaurant. You get out of the car. She is still sitting in the car, showing no urgency to exit. You, not assessing the situation for what it's worth, wait nonchalantly on the sidewalk, thinking, *She should have had her stuff together. What is taking her so long?* Most likely she is waiting for you to open her car door and thus prove that chivalry is not dead, indeed. So, now that you have failed one of the rules governing the Gentleman's Test, all is not lost. The amount of courtesy and generosity a person may show is definitely based upon circumstances and one's willingness to learn how to treat a lady. Doing so to exemplify the real soul of a man!

Question 5
Does He/She Hold Your Hand in Public?

Ashleigh: Men hold hands because they know it pleases women and because it is the form of public affection easiest for them.

Andrew: Women like it when men to hold their hands in public because it shows others that you are a couple. Don't ask, just grab her hand. She will think it is a sweet gesture.

If he has never attempted to hold your hand, it could be for one of two reasons: either he feels uncomfortable and is waiting for you to hold his hand, or perhaps he is obsessive-compulsive and feels excessive fear of germs. Then again, there may be the problem relative to the "fear of the other woman." The truth is, a woman will test a man from time to time—if you don't attempt to hold her hand, you failed. She may reason that you don't care, that you are forgetful, or that you are not listening. Some men are simplistic in nature. They may think, *I am taking you out and we are together, so it does not matter if we hold hands or not.* However, there are some telling signs. For instance, if a man grabs a woman's hand, jerking it forcibly toward him, this could indicate that he is the controlling type.

Question 6
Is He/She Flirtatious?

◇◇◇◇◇◇◇◇◇◇◇◇◇◇◇◇◇◇◇◇◇◇◇◇◇◇◇◇◇◇◇◇

Ashleigh: Men flirt just to see if they still have what it takes to approach women. There is a very thin line between what men define as flirting and disrespect.

Andrew: Women use flirtation as a form of manipulation. To put it bluntly, flirting is a way for women to exploit men who may be naïve and giving. If not for that purpose, flirting is the aspect of dating that shows another person that we are interested without us having to say it.

Use flirting wisely; know what kind of man you are dating. Flirtation is the act of being overly friendly, and another way to attract attention.

Here's a scenario worth mentioning: A couple walks into a store and the female spots an old male friend. She approaches him, their eyes meet and they exchange a friendly hug (the kind of hug with some space between the bodies—a "church hug," if you will). He compliments her on how well she looks despite the many years that have passed. Quite coy and giggling infectiously, she asks how long he has been working there, because it is one of her favorite places to shop, and whether he receives a discount. He answers in the affirmative and places his hand on the small of her back while walking her toward the register. Noticing the muscled tone of his arms, she asks if he has been working out.

Have the vestiges of flirting taken root here? Has it even gone too far? Now, depending on who you are with, the answers to those questions are definitely going to determine the gist of this analogy. It's interesting to note that most men are okay with flirting as long as there are benefits that suggest triumph. This brings me to my next question.

Question 7
Is He/She Jealous?

∞∞∞∞∞∞∞∞∞∞∞∞∞∞∞∞∞∞∞∞∞∞∞∞

Ashleigh: A man's jealous personality, which may be caused by a lack of experience, trust or his past, defines him.

Andrew: A woman is likely to become jealous of certain behavior toward another person, if such behavior should be shared with her instead.

Jealousy is most often confused with being insecure. One should know that jealousy and insecurity are entirely different emotions.

To further illustrate this point, flirting is the quickest way to make either gender fly off into a jealous state. Moreover, when a person shares a close friendship with another person outside of their relationship, the partner will get jealous and fearful of the unknown. Thus, it is important for couples to sit down together and explain the history of their past and present friendships. Also, it is important to discuss each other's view on what may cause an uncomfortable situation. A man who feels jealous will view his partner's actions as a sign of disrespect, not as a reflection of his emotional issues. A woman who feels jealous will get upset and either walk off or punish you by withholding whatever it is that you like or want at that particular time. Women deal with the emotions for what it is right at the moment it happened.

Question 8

Has He/She Ever Cheated On Someone?

◇◇◇

Ashleigh: Men never ask this question for fear that they will be asked the same in return.

Andrew: Women ask this question to judge your character.

If men and women have been unfaithful, this is the question that they both are afraid of answering truthfully. Most men will tell a woman what she wants to hear and often deflect by asking the same question, hoping to gain an advantage. A woman's response to this question will probably be more expansive and include a detailed explanation why she has or has not cheated in the past. The way she answers will ultimately have a direct influence on the nature of the relationship, respectively whether she will continue or stop dating you. If a woman hears the answer *yes*, her response to hooking up with you is most likely *no*! Men are a lot more forgiving of a woman's response to this question, especially if they are interested in you. If the man or the women is promiscuous, this question and its answer may have no effect at all.

Question 9
Does He/She Openly Communicate?

❈❈

Ashleigh: Men are only going to tell women what they feel is important enough to mention.

Andrew: Women tell men everything, even unnecessary details.

Most men don't really like to talk about the need to communicate and feel that details are unnecessary. They feel that, as long as you understood the gist of the conversation, they have achieved their goal of effective communication. On the other hand, women feel that the worst form of neglect is the failure to communicate. Moreover, women are far more expressive and constantly talk to their partners about their feelings, problems, past experiences, and life in general, and they do so to give you insight to their behavior. A man normally will reply to anything with as few words as possible. Men's one-word answers are annoying to women. They will ask even more questions, which will eventually frustrate both parties. He will get tired of all the questions, and she will get mad that she has to ask that many questions to get the answer she needs! Effective communication is the key to a successful relationship.

Question 10
Is He/She Romantic?

✤✤✤✤✤✤✤✤✤✤✤✤✤✤✤✤✤✤✤✤✤✤✤✤✤✤✤

Ashleigh: A man's idea of a romantic date is impressing her with an expensive dinner and flowers.

Andrew: A woman knows the typical dinner-and-flowers routine. In her opinion, the real art of romance includes listening to her interests, spontaneously articulating something thoughtful, and having unique ideas.

There are certain elements that spell "romance" to a woman: music, flowers, candles, candies, lingerie, and sharing time doing something she enjoys. It's all about creating the ambiance of the moment and the mood for intimacy. Men can get all of these things right—it just does not happen as often as women would like. Romantic women, on the other hand, possess a smooth sensuousness. They are always sensitive to affection and make you feel that every time should be different. Romance, if conveyed appropriately, can be an important component that adds excitement to a relationship meant for life.

Imagine spending an eternity with each other in a routine relationship that does not offer an occasional break from the norm—a break that allows you to express genuine feelings, letting each other know that appreciation and love are synonymous, and still a factor in the relationship.

Question 11
Is He/She Conceited?

✕✕✕✕✕✕✕✕✕✕✕✕✕✕✕✕✕✕✕✕✕✕✕✕✕✕✕✕✕✕✕✕✕✕✕

Ashleigh: A man perceives a woman as conceited if she shows an air of superiority by speaking with mannerisms such as putting her nose up in the air, or wearing attire to match.

Andrew: A woman perceives a man as conceited if he boasts about his accomplishments and his abilities.

Women do not want a man in their relationship who takes more time to get ready than they do! A woman feels that it is acceptable to have a conceited male friend, because it does not directly affect her. Believe it or not, a man actually wants a woman who has a certain amount of conceit, because it might give the impression of respect and self-confidence. However, an egotistical woman, who treats others as if they were beneath her, is undesirable to a man. Such mannerisms tend to lead to disrespect. A conceited man will speak to anyone without showing disrespect, but know that when he is talking, he talks about himself!

Question 12
Is He/She Judgmental?

Ashleigh: Men seem to be more passive, often giving the impression that they just shrug off the negative and continue on their way.

Andrew: Women tend to be more defensive in nature and seem to care about the views of others. To corroborate that statement, a woman's first defense is, "I don't care what you think!" Men would readily label that as false, for sure! A rebuttal would probably be to the tune of, "If you really did not care, you would not get upset and defensive." A man tries to keep ideas simple and relate your moral judgments to the way you were raised. Both parties will pass moral judgment considering that they were taught in different environments. Women look at every situation from many angles and often try to impose their beliefs onto their partner. Men feel that women point out the myriad of problems they have with men, because of something women do not like about themselves.

Question 13
Is He/She Confident?

∞∞∞∞∞∞∞∞∞∞∞∞∞∞∞∞∞∞∞∞∞∞∞∞∞

Ashleigh: A man's view of a confident woman is of a woman of substance, who is not arrogant and does not need to be reassured. She is strong, has an air of sophistication, and possesses style and charisma.

Andrew: A woman notices confidence in a man by the swagger in the way he walks, talks, and handles business.

Confidence is not about looks. It has more to do with self-confidence and belief in oneself. No one is completely confident; we need to be comfortable and knowledgeable in an area to feel confident. If you exude a general air of confidence, people will believe anything you say and do. This is why not everyone is cut out to be, say, a car salesman. You have to possess a high level of confidence in the way you present yourself, and the way you converse with others. Confidence in a person is just another attractive characteristic for both men and women. People are drawn to positive human beings.

Question 14
Is He/She Mature?

〰〰〰〰〰〰〰〰〰〰〰〰〰〰〰

Ashleigh: A man feels that he is mature as long as he handles his responsibilities.

Andrew: Women believe that they are far more mature than men at *any* age.

Couples throw the word "immature" at each other as an insult. Why is this considered an insult, when maturity is based largely on having experience? Knowing your partner's past experiences, and how your partner handled them, will often tell you a great deal about his or her maturity level and thought processes. You can judge a person's maturity based on the way he or she handles negative emotions such as anger, jealousy, and fear. Some women will prefer dating an older man, hoping that he will be more mature than a younger man.

Question 15
Can He/She Cook?

Ashleigh: Men typically view a woman's ability to cook as a requirement. A woman who does not cook is at a disadvantage.

Andrew: Women feel that a man who can cook is attractive, because it is one less stressful chore for her.

Let's clarify the definitive value of being able to cook! Anyone can put something on the stove and attempt to cook. Being able to cook actually means that the person consuming the food you prepared considers it to be good. If the only meal you can cook exceptionally well is spaghetti and nothing else, you cannot cook! Making boxed meals, noodles, and frozen foods is not cooking, either; it is heating up something to eat. Men love a woman who can cook. For a woman to find a man who can cook, or has a passion to cook, may be like finding rest and relaxation after a hard day at work. Paradoxically, if a woman does not know how to cook, a man will try to get his female family members to teach her a thing or two in the kitchen.

Question 16
Is He/She Lazy?

<><><><><><><><><><><><><><><><>

Ashleigh: A man's definition of lazy refers to a woman who lacks continuity and the penchant for completing daily chores.

Andrew: A woman calls a man lazy if he fails to hold steady employment, or does not *want* to work.

A woman's main concern with a lazy man is his complacency when he is not astute enough to find a job and keep it.

Moreover, a woman does not really concern herself with a man doing chores, because she will most likely just redo his work and fix it to her liking. Although a woman may complain that the man does nothing in the house, the complaint is really about his lack of appreciation. It would be nice for a man to do a chore or two without being asked. From the male perspective, it is a woman's responsibility to take care of the home, and when she doesn't do her job, he considers her lazy.

Can He/She Read?

✧✧✧✧✧✧✧✧✧✧✧✧✧✧✧✧✧✧✧✧✧✧✧

Ashleigh: A man will not tolerate women who do not read, let alone those who cannot read.

Andrew: If a woman has found a good man, she will stick with him, regardless of his shortcomings.

Despite all the technology in the world, sadly, there are still adults who cannot read. This can pose a great strain on a relationship because it is teaching a language. Anyone who has ever taught school knows that one must have patience. A man wants a woman who can handle quite a bit of responsibility. Not being able to read can pose a serious threat to all of the duties that one must perform. If one cannot read, certain routine errands such as helping the kids with homework, following an instruction manual or driving directions, are near impossible. If a woman is in love, she will take on the challenge.

Question 18
Is He/She Selfish?

◇◇◇◇◇◇◇◇◇◇◇◇◇◇◇◇◇◇◇◇◇◇◇◇◇◇◇◇◇◇

Ashleigh: Men feel that women are very selfish and only think about what they want, but don't realize what they are asking of their men.

Andrew: Women feel that men are selfish because they are set in their ways and will not compromise in a relationship.

Selfishness is always thinking about oneself. Men seem to believe that women fit this category like a pair of favorite shoes. Men feel that women constantly nag them to change, hoping that they'll become what the women want them to be. The problem is, a man will change one thing, hoping that the woman will leave him alone, but when the woman realizes that her nagging worked, she will start nagging him about changing the next thing on her list. The man gets tired, gives up, and does not want to compromise with the woman.

Women need to appreciate their partners and strive for needs, not wants, in the relationship. Women feel that men take the things women do for men for granted and act selfish. Women can do a lot to foster compatibility in relationships. Women can appreciate their partners and strive for benefits that help to combat selfish attitudes, which stem from perceiving that men take them for granted.

Question 19
Is He/She Sensitive?

Ashleigh: A man thinks being sensitive means showing vulnerability. He can't let that happen, because a tough front must be maintained at all times.

Andrew: A woman wants a man to be sensitive, to be able to express feelings, and to show enough emotion to shed a tear or two.

Women are really curious to see if men experience the same variety of emotions that they do. The A man must show sensitivity in moderation, with the propensity for emotional release. Otherwise women will lose respect and will no longer be attracted to him. The trick is to give her the sensitive emotion she craves and not lose masculine fortitude. To add to this, men should show more affection, acquiesce to watching movies of her choice, and give her compliments as needed.

Question 20
Is He/She Self-Sufficient?

∞∞∞∞∞∞∞∞∞∞∞∞∞∞∞∞∞∞∞∞∞∞∞∞∞

Ashleigh: A man feels better believing that his woman can't survive without him. This allows him to have a sense of purpose.

Andrew: A woman does not like a man who is dependent upon her for everything. It shows weakness and a lack of initiative.

Since the dawn of time, men have been responsible for hunting and providing for women. A man is not concerned if a woman can provide for herself, but he will definitely attempt pulling more than his own weight. A man is most uncomfortable when a woman makes more money than he does, no matter how much he may brag to his friends about his woman's success, reassuring everyone that her success is not a problem. Self-sufficiency is being confident enough to know that if your woman or your man should leave you, you can definitely make it on your own! Do not put all of your eggs in one basket!

Question 21
Does He/She Have Any Children?

Ashleigh: When children are involved, compatibility is always a point of contention in a harmonious relationship. Case in point: A man will accept a woman who has a child or children if he does, too, but if he is single without kids, he would prefer a single woman without kids.

Andrew: A woman is not particularly crazy about dating a man with a child or children, even if she has children, too.

The problem with a single woman having no kids but dating a man with kids is "baby mama drama." This is highlighted by the fact that a woman does not want to deal with a man's past, knowing that he had children with another woman. A single man does not like to get involved with a single woman with kids, because he fears that he may be forced to be father to another man's children. This problem seems even more serious to men, if the children exhibit a lack of discipline or control. This creates a difficult situation with the potential for dire consequences. This situation can drive men mad, because they don't want to get involved with taking disciplinary action for fear of conflict in the relationship to the children's mother. When kids are involved in a new relationship, the realm of the unknown is magnified, and having to end the relationship is potentially heartbreaking for all concerned. Men and women should avoid certain situations and keep things simple, if kids by one or the other partner might be a problem to a successful union.

Question 22
Does He/She Have Negative Habits?

∞∞∞∞∞∞∞∞∞∞∞∞∞∞∞∞∞∞∞∞∞∞∞∞∞∞∞∞∞∞∞∞∞∞∞

Ashleigh: A man will overlook whatever habits you have, if they don't have an effect on the relationship.

Andrew: A woman may date a man with a bad habit, but she will look for opportunities to change him for the better.

Mannerisms pertaining to habits are important in any relationship. Honesty and disclosure of anything that might impede progress or hinder compatibility often spell the difference between success and failure in a relationship. Negative habits are habits that later in life prove to be detrimental to your health. There are quite a few situations that are proven facts. For instance, smoking can cause poor physical fitness, lung cancer, and emphysema; excessive drinking affects the brain, heart, and muscles and may lead to cancer as well.

When you meet someone, watch his or her normal partake relative to what has been ascribed above to help determine if it would be problematic to the relationship. Have the temerity of mind to talk about any bad habits, real or imagined, for approval or disapproval. From a man's point of view, women have been known to enter into relationships, thinking that they can change a person's ways, but conventional wisdom says that they might be setting themselves up for failure. Old habits die hard, and rarely do they go away without a concerted and determined effort to quit outright. People will only quit if they truly want to and are ready to deal with the consequences. There are so many people in a relationships who have promised that they will quit drinking or smoking but haven't. Instead, they may hide all traces of the habit that may be detrimental in the future.

Question 23
Does He/She Have Any Diseases?

◇◇◇

Ashleigh: A man may fail to tell a woman that he has a disease, because he doesn't want her to worry, or because he does not want her to show sympathy.

Andrew: A woman may fail to tell a man about her disease right away, because she does not want to be rejected. She may be waiting for the right time in the conversation to discuss it.

There are many devastating diseases in the world that can cause havoc in viable relationships. Knowing if your partner has any diseases such as hypertension, cancer or heart disease is important. Some people do not know how to treat or help someone who is experiencing potentially fatal symptoms. Your partner may fail to mention a common disease like diabetes, because he or she thinks that it is under control. Whether the illness is severe or minor, it is important to establish meaningful communication about the potential danger signs. If you fail to disclose information regarding your illness, your partner may feel deceived and hurt, which will create unnecessary trust issues.

Question 24
Is he/she employed?

<hr>

Ashleigh: A man doesn't mind if a woman has a job as long as it does not affect the household or his job.

Andrew: A woman looks for a man who is employed, because of the many wondrous possibilities.

Men prefer women who work, because this means that they don't have to spend all of their money. A man does not want a woman to work in a job that requires her to do excess physical labor. He wants to see her work somewhere behind a desk in corporate America. If she is not working, she is most likely at home with the kids. This is the only acceptable time for a woman to be unemployed.

Question 25
Does He/She Own a Vehicle?

Ashleigh: A man feels it is critical to have a vehicle.

Andrew: A woman doesn't feel having a vehicle is that important, if her man has a vehicle she can drive.

A woman does not like to be second behind a man's love for his car. A working vehicle with a full tank of gas spells freedom to both genders. However, men seem to take more pride in their vehicles than women. Women take the necessary precautions to ensure that their vehicles continues to run, like the occasional tune-up and oil change. Men, however, take caring for their vehicles to another level—the "accessory" level, which involves what women like to call a "man's toys." These accessories are the tires, rims, stereo systems, televisions, back-up cameras, and the like. Men who buy expensive vintage vehicles are most likely going to spend a lot of time with or bragging about their car collection. A woman only cares about a vehicle when it is time to go out or when the vehicle has stopped working!

Does He/She Use a Lot of Profanity?

Ashleigh: A man feels that a woman should always act like a lady, and therefore the excessive use of profanity is not attractive.

Andrew: A woman does not care if her man uses profanity as long as it is not directed at her.

Many men believe that a woman has to carry herself like a lady and should let men handle problems. When a man uses profanity in a woman's defense, the woman will think that he is behaving in a manly way. It has always been viewed that it is okay for a man to use profanity and that woman should remain tight-lipped. The only time it is acceptable for a woman to use profanity is in his defense or out of anger. Nowadays, profanity is part of everyday vernacular.

Whether or not you use profanity, it is a choice not a rule.

Question 27
Is He/She Cheap?

∞∞∞∞∞∞∞∞∞∞∞∞∞∞∞∞∞∞∞∞

Ashleigh: A man who is cheap makes it obvious, no matter what his actions are. He may comment on prices, and it may show in his appearance.

Andrew: A woman wants and needs far too many hygiene and personal products for her to be cheap.

There is a huge difference between shopping cost-effectively and being just plain cheap. This is a huge problem for a woman because, if he is cheap, she cannot expect anything that might require him spending more than he is be willing to shell out. A cheap man is not going to spend his money on flowers that may die a week later. Instead, he will buy you something useful, something like new towels or slippers to prevent you from walking on the carpet in your shoes.

A woman is not normally called cheap, if cheap means being reluctant to spend frivolously. In some cases the opposite is true, and she is a compulsive spender! A tight spender, or anyone who is cost-effective, will only buy things he or she needs as opposed to what he or she wants.

A woman will pay full price for her personal needs, where a man will buy an off-brand or no-frills product if it is cheaper.

Is He/She Family Orientated?

Ashleigh: A man does not care if you have a good or bad relationship with your family as long as it doesn't interfere with your relationship.

Andrew: A woman does not want a "mama's boy," but she would prefer that her man have respect for his family.

Women believe that family morals and the way a man treats his family will tell them how they will treat women. This is a misconception to a degree, because a man only expects certain things, such as loyalty, support, and praise from his family. A person only puts a certain amount of faith into each individual in the family, knowing what they can expect form that person. Also, when it is time to meet the family, everyone is nice to you. An overprotective and nosey mother is a problem and can be disastrous to your relationship. Truth is, no matter how much we love someone, seeking family approval is important. If the family doesn't approve of your partner, it can cause strain on a relationship, especially during holidays. The desire to be with each other on the holidays can also be challenging, if you've decided not to visit each other's family.

Question 29
How Old Is He/She?

Ashleigh: A man does not care how old a woman is as long as she is of a legal age agreeable to both.

Andrew: A woman prefers to date someone her age, or someone a few years older.

Age is important, because looks can be deceiving, and dating a minor is against the law. Most men approach women with, "I hope you don't mind me asking your age, because you look kind of young?" Although this may be a compliment, he is also covering his ass. When people don't ask, one word comes to mind—pedophile! Neither a male nor a female should be uncomfortable asking or giving a person their real age. Truth is, no one is going to ask to see identification. Older men seem to enjoy dating younger ladies for their pleasure and excitement. Women are dating much older men, because they are established, rich, or influential in the social strata.

Question 30
Does He/She Invade Your Privacy?

Ashleigh: A man feels that going through his belongings, including cell phones, when he is not around is an invasion of privacy.

Andrew: Privacy issues are not a concern for most women, because they feel that anything really important should not be positioned for easy discovery. Most men would not bother to search!

Men can't stand having someone going through their personal items, because it shows a lack of trust. Women feel it is their right to look through their men's personal belongings, especially if they have nothing to hide. Both parties in a relationship should consider this: if you leave your e-mail open, your significant other will look, because curiosity will prevail. It is almost human nature for a woman to want to know what is going on in her man's life, regardless of any form of insecurity. So, does she invade your privacy? Damn right! If men were not so secretive, women would not be so nosey.

Question 31

Has He/She Ever Had an Alcohol or Drug Abuse Problem?

Ashleigh: A man is more supportive of a woman, who once had or currently has a substance abuse problem.

Andrew: A woman can only help so much, before she becomes depressed or falls victim to the abuser.

This question is going to take a bit of investigating because of the nature of sensitivity. No one wants to be judged about their past knowing that their past behavior is still important. How long someone has been sober or clean matters, because it determines whether or not the addiction could possibly be a future issue. Thus, it is essential to learn about the genesis of the abuse problem. Is the person taking preventative measures? If the person began using to deal with the stress of everyday life, entering into a relationship might not be the best idea. No one can prevent all stressful situations. Therefore, a new relationship may initiate continued negative behavior. If you chose to become involved (in a relationship) knowing the circumstances, you'd basically succumb to the fact that you must help that person cope. You would not give up on them, because you have given much thought to the situation before ultimately choosing that path.

Question 32

Does He/She Have Sex
on the First Date?

∞∞∞∞∞∞∞∞∞∞∞∞∞∞∞∞∞∞∞∞∞∞∞∞∞∞∞∞∞

Ashleigh: A man will want to have sex on the first date. If he doesn't, he shows himself to be a gentleman.

Andrew: If circumstances are favorable, and if she is attracted to you, a woman will have sex on the first date. If she doesn't, she may be looking at the bigger picture and hoping for a sustained relationship.

A man will view a woman as "easy" if she gives it up on the first date. Women have ways of testing a situation after sex on the first date. She invariably may ask a question relative to his opinion of her, and his reply will determine the nature of future interaction. It should be noted that, in most cases, women hold the power with regards to whether or not sexual relations will take place. If she is looking for a husband, she will not have sex on the first date, because the man and other spectators may possibly judge her negatively. One-night-stands are encounters during which both men and women let physical attraction get the best of them. Either party may practice abstinence on religious or spiritual grounds.

Question 33
Does He/She Kiss on the First Date?

Ashleigh: A man feels that there shouldn't be any time lost when taking the initiative to kiss right away.

Andrew: A woman feels that kissing will tell her whether there's physical attraction or chemistry. She may also kiss to satisfies her curiosity.

When a woman first realizes that she likes a man, the first thought that crosses her mind is, "I wonder if he can kiss?" A man will go for a kiss hoping that she won't turn her head. If they commence the kiss, the man believes that feelings are mutual. Hopefully there will be another date. On the other hand, a woman on a date takes the man for a test drive, and a kiss will determine which direction she wants to go. Women are looking for any emotional aspect to help them determine the level of commitment (to the man) after the first kiss. If she is attracted to you, a good kiss will seal the deal on the first date.

Question 34

Does He/She Share the Same Sexual Drive?

Ashleigh: A man will feel neglected if a woman does not indulge in sex as often as he would like.

Andrew: A woman's sexual drive is really determined by her mood. If she is negatively affected by stress, a crisis, or financial difficulties, her sexual drive will be very low.

Libido is important to both genders. Men and women experience sexual peeks at different times, but as each year passes, one percent of the male and female hormones decrease. Most women will say that men have a much stronger sexual drive than women, but it is not the sexual drive that has men sleeping with various partners, it is the excitement of something new. In a day, a man will compensate for what you don't give him by masturbating. A man's sexual drive can be low, but if a woman wants to have sex, the man will still please her. A woman controls how often her man gets laid! The excuses—I have a headache, I am tired, I had a bad day, and I don't feel well—all really mean the same thing—I am not in the mood!

Question 35
Does He/She Have a Criminal Record?

Ashleigh: To a man, as long as a woman has not committed murder, he doesn't care. In fact, he feels superior.

Andrew: A woman wants to know the gritty details of the case, the situation, and your current opinion on the matter.

There are a series of questions that pertain to crimes. Men with controlling attitudes have been known to throw temper tantrums and *exhibit* streaks of violence, similar to Ike Turner's behavior toward Tina. A man is not worried if a woman has a record for violence, because men try to be non-confrontational anyway. Men are not going to start a fight, because it would interrupt Sports Center.

Men are known to be the physically abusive gender, and that's why women are careful when dating. If the crime was possession, a woman wants to know if you abused the substance, or if you were just caught trafficking it. A woman will have an easier time to let her guard down if the crime seemed to be just, like self-defense or wrongful identity. But a past crime may still cause a lack of trust.

Question 36
What Is His/Her Religion?

Ashleigh: A man would rather a woman conform to his religion, because it is difficult to start over.

Andrew: A woman would be willing to convert to another religion for the sake of the relationship.

You can learn a lot about a person's behavior and traditions regarding religion and spiritual upbringing. Religious beliefs can be traced to mannerisms and behavior patterns. For example, a Catholic's prayer and confession to the Lord atones his or her sins. Buddhists believe in enlightenment obtained through righteous conduct, inner wisdom, and meticulous meditation. Being of a different religion should not affect the decision as to whether to date someone. Religions are fraught with very interesting conversation pieces, may spur debates, and provide learning experiences. Therefore, it is extremely important for the sake of the relationship to respect certain traditions, even if your own belief is different. Insulting the beliefs of one religion in favor of another is the surest way to start an argument. When you've decided to date or even start a family, it is more important that you discuss which religion you will practice as a family.

Question 37
What Is His/Her Racial Make-up?

Ashleigh: Men are far more explorative than women, because they don't carry excess baggage or fear when trying something new.

Andrew: Women worry about all aspects of dating and would rather stick to what they know makes them feel most comfortable.

Women dissect every situation; they worry about what others think and might say. Coming from different backgrounds is normally only a problem to those who tend to compare your relationship to close families and friends. Status, location, and the way you were raised will tell a person whether or not crossing racial lines will cause a conflict in a relationship. No one truly knows what and how another ethnic group suffers from stereotypical mindsets and perceptions in the world.

Situations will not get better until you step out of your own race and date someone of different persuasion. You will realize that before everyone participates in some form of racial stereotyping. Most people believe that they can't help whom they fall in love with, regardless of race or background. It all goes back to the story of "Romeo and Juliet": you taste the forbidden fruit out of curiosity and then decide whether you are a good fit for a relationship. However, being from the same background has its advantages for a relationship: certain issues will be understood without having to speak on them.

Question 38

What Are His/Her Interests?

×××

Ashleigh: A man has limits with regards to the woman's interests he is willing to share. For instance, a man is not going to take up knitting!

Andrew: Women really just want to know that you genuinely care about what she does and likes; you don't necessarily have to learn how to do it. It's the thought that counts.

Often a shared interest depends on either how you met, or what attracted you to that special someone in the first place. It is fun, and can add friendly competition to the relationship. Being able to enjoy interests common to both parties will keep the relationship fresh. Invariably, if the person you are going to date is not interested or willing to try anything that you enjoy, the relationship will probably fail! Sharing common interests is important, yet there may need to be some compromise. Open your mind to try new adventures; it can be an exciting learning experience. If he does not like cold climates but you love to ski, try taking up water skiing together. Happy mediums are important, because relationships are all about spending quality time with each other by merging your interests and lifestyle.

Question 39

Is His/Her Residence Long Distance?

Ashleigh: Men prefer not to get into long distance relationships, because local relationships are more convenient.

Andrew: A woman will sacrifice and travel to visit her man.

Men cope with long distance relationships far better than women. Men go on with their scheduled events and remain busy. They're out of sight, out of mind. A woman finds it hard to keep her man interested and makes the most effort to ensure that the relationship is steady. Being involved in a long distance relationship is a huge responsibility, and there are certain things you must do for it to work: making the phone calls, sending packages, writing letters, and setting aside that quality time. A man will normally make a schedule for himself based on his availability. A woman will use all means possible just to send a note, or correspond accordingly. Both parties have to deal with the repeated goodbyes after each visit, and both parties have to handle the temptation that haunts you, placing fear and doubt into your mind. You only have your mind to share over the phone, and now it is corrupt with negative thoughts.

Question 40
What Is His/Her Living Arrangement?

<hr>

Ashleigh: A man does not care about your living arrangements as long as there is enough privacy for solitary fortitude.

Andrew: A woman cares where and how you live and who you live with!

A woman does not like it if a man is still living at home with his parents. If he is living at home, she wants to know why. She also wants to know his future goals. She understands if a man is living with a roommate, but she does not feel comfortable with it, because it means that her privacy will be compromised, and that she cannot move about freely.

To her, the old adage "cleanliness is next to godliness" holds sway when it comes to an orderly coexistence. If he has a roommate, the person must be of the same sex. Men could care less and find the aforementioned less of a problem.

Question 41
Is He/She Fond of Animals?

Ashleigh: A man views animals as pets and as another responsibility.

Andrew: A woman views animals not as pets but as companions.

For most women who love pets, cats and dogs are considered part of the family. Women love, nurture, and protect their animals. Men buy animals for females because they are aware that they will occupy the woman's time and be her companion. Most women who have a dog often feel as if their animal is more affectionate than their partner. Often the relationship between a dog and a woman who loves pets is similar to her relationship with a man. Men prefer dominant male dogs, thus adding to the saying that a dog is a man's best friend, especially if the dog protects the home in his absence.

Question 42
Does He/She Have Any Surgical Implants, Cosmetic Surgeries or Other Artificial Body Parts?

◇◇

Ashleigh: A man will most likely not date, or avoid dating a woman who has body parts that are not part of her original makeup, including handicaps.

Andrew: A woman feels that a man can compensate for the fact that he has missing or artificial limbs.

Men dislike explaining to friends and family certain things about their relationship and partner. They would rather avoid the awkwardness of the situation and dismiss the person. On the other hand, a woman would be willing to date a man who has artificial body parts. Especially if he is really nice, has great

personality traits, and money. These things could compensate for any shortcomings alluding to his handicaps. This may sound shallow, but caring for a handicapped adult is a responsibility, and many women may feel less enthused about missing limbs and artificial joints. Both men and women feel it is imperative to discuss any changes you may have made to your body since birth. It is best to discuss gender reassignment, dual genitalia, and deformities.

Is He/She Indulging in Protected Sex?

Ashleigh: A man feels that a woman always expects him to be prepared to use protection, but that she rarely provides protection for him.

Andrew: A woman has no problem asking a man if he has protection before they have intercourse.

A man will only do what a woman allows him to do. A woman feels that if she does not ask a man to use protection, he will normally have no problem having sex without it. It is both parties' responsibility to provide and wear protection during intercourse. There are many questions concerning their use: Yes, the sensation is different depending on whether you have sex with or without condoms, but is contracting a disease or conceiving a baby worth taking the risk? Are the consequences of your actions worth that one moment of pleasure? If a woman has unprotected sex, she is alarmed and will wonder about the possibility of a pregnancy until her menstrual cycle resumes.

Has He/She Ever Been Tested for HIV/AIDS?

∞∞∞∞∞∞∞∞∞∞∞∞∞∞∞∞∞∞∞∞∞∞∞∞∞∞∞∞∞∞

Ashleigh: Most men will probably not ask this question, because they are afraid that their question may seem out of line and offensive.

Andrew: A woman is most likely to ask this question, because she knows how important health is for a family. Moreover, she doesn't want an illness to affect her ability to have children.

AIDS/HIV is a very touchy subject, because there are no visible signs, and no one can tell whether or not anyone is infected. If you ask this question, many will think that you have AIDS/HIV, or that you've had a scare and are more cautious now. No one should be offended or upset if someone asks this question. If you are taking care of yourself and are adamantly sure that you're clean, being tested should not be an issue and can be part of your annual check-up. If you are sexually active with many partners, then it should be incumbent of you to get tested on a frequent basis.

Getting tested can be very scary. Most people don't know that a person could live symptom-free for years before they find out they are ill. In those years you may infect others because you thought you were clean! Get tested, your life and the lives of others may depend on it.

Question 45

Does He/She Constantly Complain?

Ashleigh: Men hardly complain. They make subtle comments with little to no explanation and expect women to understand.

Andrew: Women complain because they are constantly expressing their feelings about the same subject, without receiving an answer to their question or a solution to their problem.

The problem is the lack to effective communication.

When a woman complains "at" a man, he automatically shuts off his receptors and turns on the automatic "okay"! When a woman hears a man respond with "okay," she thinks she has made her point. However, "okay" really means "Now I can get back to what I was doing." The problem is, a woman talks *at* her man rather than *with* her man. It is all in the approach. Instead of yelling all your complaints about what he is or is not doing, ask politely, not sarcastically, if you may have fifteen minutes of his time to speak with him uninterrupted. Women, any more time than that is fraught with danger—no one wants to sit through a long lecture about faults, problems, and shortcomings. Do not place all the blame on one person; it takes two people to effectively communicate.

Question 46
Does He/She Have a Life-Altering Secret?

✕✕✕

Ashleigh: Men have a propensity to hide financial burdens and quickly reveal a personal secret.

Andrew: A woman will probably wait to tell her secret until she is either sure she can trust you, or until she knows you are in love with her.

Intimate, if not personal information held close to the vest should be revealed early in the dating game, because levels of deceit can cause disharmony in the relationship. So-called secrets such as having had a sex change, not being able to have kids, being terminally ill, can change both partners' lives. A woman may want to wait longer than a man to reveal her secret, because she fears it may affect her lifestyle.

You can't trust that logic, because you are giving someone the courtesy of knowing your secret. The key to it all is being in a position to counter behavior patterns when the secret is out, making sure they won't cause a scene or worse, tell others. Also, the fear of rejection is psychologically traumatizing and painful. It is the fear of starting over and over, trying to find someone who can handle and look past your secret. Men will handle secrets, if no deception is involved. A woman feels that she has a better chance if she waits until the man loves her enough not to leave.

Question 47
Does He/She Have Good Personal Hygiene?

◇◇◇◇◇◇◇◇◇◇◇◇◇◇◇◇◇◇◇◇◇◇◇◇◇◇◇◇◇◇◇◇◇◇◇◇◇◇◇

Ashleigh: Men expect women to always have good personal hygiene, especially since women have a menstrual cycle.

Andrew: To a woman, a man's hygiene is the first impression!

Good personal hygiene includes brushing your teeth twice a day, showering daily, wearing deodorant, and maintaining a well-groomed appearance. Keep the main areas fresh. To the average woman, aspects of good personal hygiene are a good set of teeth, no bad breath and no unpleasant body odors. A man will work with a woman if she has semi-good hygiene, and hint at what he likes, and buy her what is necessary. Men want women who shave their legs, underarms, and bikini zone. They like women who match their undergarments and maintain their new look. Hair, nails, and feet must be in good condition, too. A person's hygiene will give you indication as to how they maintain their house and property.

Question 48
Does He/She Have Trust Issues?

Ashleigh: A man will trust until a woman has broken his trust.

Andrew: A man has to gain a woman's trust before she will trust him.

Proving to be trustworthy and maintaining it throughout a relationship can be difficult if past issues continue to spill over into the present. Women want men to prove that they have earned their trust, but men give their portion of trust upfront and deal with issues as they arise. A man will get tired of being accused of wrong-doing, because a woman does not trust him. It can cause a man to cheat or withdraw intimacy. Gaining trust is hard for both partners, because they both have to rely on someone else's strength to protect feelings of insecurity. Trusting your partner means that you are placing confidence in him or her, expecting your partner to show integrity by respecting and caring for you. Trust is a powerful ingredient in any relationship. Gain someone's trust and maintain it!

Question 49
Is He/She Understanding?

Ashleigh: Men feel that they are understanding if they listen, don't forget about memorable experiences, and do as women ask.

Andrew: A woman wants a man to take the effort and time to really get to know her, not only on the surface but also deep within her. A woman does not want to spell it out every single time. She wants her emotions and actions understood.

There is a monumental difference between knowing someone and understanding someone. Anyone can learn facts such birthdays or favorite foods and say, "I *know* that person." Making an earnest effort to firmly communicate what your intentions are to another person, and that person grasping the essence of what you're conveying—that is understanding in the true sense of the word. If a female tells her partner that she was raped by a close male friend, you should be able to grasp how she must have felt to be deceived by someone so close—without her saying anything further. This would bring you closer to understanding why her behavior toward intimacy might be negative. She does not want sympathy, nor does she want your reassurance that you will not do the same; she wants you to understand her behavior and be patient.

Question 50

Is He/She Ready to Commit?

Ashleigh: A man will not commit to anyone if he is not ready. A forced commitment is not in the best interests of a sustainable and successful relationship.

Andrew: A woman wants her man to commit, no matter whether it is to a relationship or a marriage, because commitment enhances her safety net.

Most men don't want to commit, because the idea of permanence takes away their sense of freedom, tying them to one person. When a man is ready to commit, he will enforce certain changes on his own. Men and women have pre-conceived notions of the behavior patterns that are acceptable in marriages as opposed to a relationship. After a woman dedicates a certain amount of years to her man, she feels that she deserves to be made an "honest woman." Why buy the milk, when you can get the cow for free? This is how women feel about commitment. A woman who is not ready to commit is full of doubt and fear, and until she can place those emotions aside, a successful marriage is unlikely. Commitment includes agreement on what is acceptable and tolerated in the relationship, and good communication enabling the longer haul. You'd have to ask yourself: do you believe this person or that person is going to be with you forever, being faithful, respectful, communicating, compromising, and loving? The ability to love someone despite past (or present) imperfections defines true love. If any of the above is true for you, you can truly commit and be committed.

One must realize that your definition of a word or answer to a question may be different from someone else's definition or answer. The major reasons for failed marriages and relationships are: lack of communication, money, failed expectations, and/or unmet needs! Take some time out of your busy schedules and sit down with your partner, asking and listening to the questions and answers about each other. Then, coexist for a few months and see if feelings have changed over. You will notice that when you first discussed the questions, you may not have been quite open with one another, or may not have been honest about your feelings. When you first start to date someone, you don't want to come off as judgmental, or too forceful in your opinions. Time is the best barometer for gauging what you have learned about the person, and for observing the direction of the relationship. After a few disagreements, the lines of communication may have a little blockage, and asking questions can be a prominent way to help with your problems.

Investigate

1. Is he/she single?

2. Does he/she have a child or children?

3. What is his/her living arrangement?

4. Does he/she live local or long distance?

5. What is his/her educational background?

6. Is he/she employed?

7. Is he/she bisexual, gay, or lesbian?

8. Is he/she an honest person?

9. Does he/she share the same cultural background?

10. Can he/she cook?

11. Does he/she have animals?

12. Does he/she know how to read?

13. Does he/she wear contacts?

14. Does he/she have any artificial body parts?

15. Has he/she ever committed a misdemeanor or felony?

16. Does he/she have any life altering secrets?

Dating Interests

17. Does he/she like politics?

18. Does he/she enjoy the same music?

19. Does he/she like the same sports?

20. Does he/she enjoy watching television?

21. Does he/she like going to the theater?

22. Does he/she like to travel?

23. Does he/she enjoy reading books?

24. Does he/she like the beach?

25. Does he/she dislike any certain climate?

26. Does he/she share the same religion?

27. Does he/she have a sense of spirituality?

28. Is he/she proud of his/her culture?

29. Does he/she respect other cultures?

30. Does he/she drink?

31. Does he/she chew or smoke?

32. Does he/she bite his/her nails?

33. Does he/she make strange noises while sleeping?

34. Does he/she sleep walk?

35. Does he/she have any bad habits?

Personality

36. Does he/she have integrity?

37. Is he/she conceited?

38. Is he/she confident?

39. Does he/she work hard?

40. Is he/she lazy?

41. Does he/she have good moral values?

42. Is he/she mature?

43. Is he/she realistic?

44. Is he/she thoughtful?

45. Is he/she romantic?

46. Is he/she flirtatious?

47. Is he/she consistent?

48. Is he/she friendly?

49. Is he/she polite?

50. Is he/she kind?

51. Is he/she funny?

52. Is he/she selfish?

53. Is he/she sensitive?

54. Does he/she adapt to different social surroundings?

55. Does he/she have a sense of humor?

Integration

56. Is he/she attentive to the needs of others?

57. Is he/she proud to be with you?

58. Is he/she on time?

59. Is he/she a non-violent person?

60. Is he/she physically compatible?

61. Is he/she attractive?

62. Is he/she willing to compromise?

63. Is he/she patient?

64. Is he/she overly dramatic?

65. Is he/she socially conscience?

66. Is he/she judgmental?

67. Is he/she able to show affection?

68. Does he/she respect others?

69. Is he/she consistently seeking to improve?

70. Is he/she passionate about anything?

71. Does he/she have a hobby?

72. Does he/she share the same sexual drive?

73. Does he/she consider other people's feelings?

74. Is he/she supportive?

Communication

75. Does he/she openly communicate?

76. Does he/she admit mistakes?

77. Is he/she able to peacefully talk through issues?

78. Is he/she able to respectively disagree?

79. Does she use a lot of profanity?

80. Is he/she able to make sound decisions?

81. Is he/she an understanding person?

82. Is he/she opinionated?

83. Is he/she able to be serious when necessary?

Hygiene

84.   Does he/she have good hygiene?

85.   Does he/she take care of his/her wardrobe?

86.   Does he/she take pride in his/her appearance?

87.   Does he/she take care of his/her body?

88.   Does he/she wash his/her hands before eating?

89.   Does he/she use lotion?

90.   Does he/she brush his/her teeth at least twice a day?

91.   Are his/her fingernails clean?

92.   Does he/she wash his/her hair often enough?

93.   Does he/she have false teeth?

Support

94. Is he/she able to make you feel better?

95. Is he/she able to accept your imperfections?

96. Does he/she push you if needed?

97. Is he/she interested in what you like to do?

98. Is he/she emotionally supportive of your decisions?

99. Is he/she willing to make necessary sacrifices?

100. Is he/she financially supportive?

101. Is he/she financially responsible?

102. Is he/she able to prioritize?

103. Does he/she own a home?

104. Does he/she own a vehicle?

105. Does he/she have fair to good credit?

106. Is he/she employed?

107. Is he/she self-sufficient?

108. Is he/she cheap?

109. Does he/she want children?

110. Is he/she goal oriented?

111. Is he/she family orientated?

112. Does he/she have a good relationship with family?

113. Does he/she have good relationships with friends?

114. Does he/she share some of the same friends?

115. Is his/her family loyal?

116. Is he/she influenced by family?

117. Is he/she influenced by friends?

118. Does he/she have a good relationship with my family?

119. Does he/she have a good relationship with my friends?

120. Does he/she have strong family values?

121. Does he/she have high self-esteem?

122. Does he/she have self-respect?

Health

123. Does he/she have any diseases?

124. Does he/she have a history of disease in the family?

125. Does he/she take any medication?

126. Does he/she use recreational drugs?

127. Does he/she have any allergies?

128. Does he/she work out or exercise?

129. Does he/she have the ability to procreate?

130. Has he/she ever attempted suicide?

Past

131. Does he/she have sex on the first date?

132. Does he/she kiss on the first date?

133. Is he/she carrying baggage from past relationships?

134. How did his/her past relationships end?

135. Does he/she use protection?

136. Has he/she ever been tested for HIV/AIDS?

137. Does he/she have a past history of family violence?

Are You Ready to Commit?

Questions For Her

1.   Is she wearing a weave?

2.   Does she visit a spa?

3.   Does she like flowers?

4.   Does she like candy or chocolate?

5.   Does she walk around commando?

6.   Does she shave her arms, legs and bikini area?

7.   Does she douche?

8.   Does she have weight issues?

9.   Has she ever been sexually assaulted?

Questions For Him

1.   Is he wearing a toupee?

2.   Does he masturbate?

3.   Does he have a receding hairline?

4.   Does he take penis enhancers or enlargers?

5.   Does he take steroids?

6.   Does he have hair growth issues?

7.   Is he a cross-dresser?

8.   Does he play video games?

9.   Has he ever been sexually assaulted?

Reviewer Remarks

El reconocimiento del lider a esos corazones ansiosos de comida sabrosa, la comida nose s mas que la representacion del cuerpo y la sangre de Jesus.

Se puede ser lider espiritual solamente?

Creeemos que no'. Un lider en la tierra es un lider de hombres, el es otro hombre, que se puede diferenciar por sus caracteristicas de conducir.

El lider es un conductor, un guia que hace comprender primero que elementos va a utilizar para guiar a su grupo al camino corrccto.

El tiene la obligacion de saber hacerse entender e interpreter, el no puede pensar que los demas lo deben esntender a el.

El debe entender a los demas y traducer el mensaje de cada persona en una comida sana, con vitaminas y rica para el paladar transmita el mensaje al cerebro y quede guardao para siempre.

Si utilizamos mucha sal, podemos arruinar un comida y producer un malestar en el aparato digestive de las personas. Si le agrgamos poca sal y el sabor pasa totalmente desapercibido, es que no encontramos el punto justo para sazonar.

El lider, entonces va a probar primero esa comida y la va a recomendar, o no' si no tiene el sabor perfecto.

Asi, sal como producto milenario, al alcance de todos y con un gran poder de saborizar, el lider debe estar al alcance de todos, con el conociemiento, porque el conocimiento sobre todas las cosas tambien es poder.

El lider debe saber saborizar en el momento justo.

El lider que conoce el punto justo para esa sal, ese toque en la vida de los demas, es muchas veces el llamado de salvacion.

Pero, que debe reconocer el lider prmero, antes de lanzar sus mensajes de sabores en la vida. Consideramos que debe ante todo reconocer a Dios.

Segundo una comunicacion permanente con Dios, no es ni mas ni menos, dar testimonio en cada acto diario.

Tercero saber escuchar. Muchos lideres no saben escuchar la voz de Dios, que en muchas oportunidades Dios le habla por medio de otros hombres y tal vez con un lenguaje poco claro, poco colloquial y para nada cultural.

Dios le esta hablando en ese hombre al lider para saber si este lo escucha, y le habla de la forma que menos el lider espera. Pore so el lider debe estar siempre preparado para escuchar y recnocer la voz de Dios.

Dios a quienes queremos ser Lideres, nos habla y se manifiesta en todo momento.

Muchas veces nosostros no lo sabemos escuchar y lo peor es que muchas veces no queremos escuchar.

Un pastor es un lider, que hace un buien pastor, por supuesto cuida a sus ovejas, y que mas, bien les da' un sitio seguro para descansar, y que mas, bien, le da' sus alimentos en los horarios apropiados del dia. Si, pero que mas, bueno tambien el pastor proteje a sus ovejas de las tempestades, de los vientos fuertes y cuida que ninguna oveja se extravie.

Entonces el lider: Alimenta, guia, proteje, y cuida que ninguno de sus discipulos se aleje del camino de Dios. Esa es la mas fuerte apuesta para el lider: Que nadie se aleje de Dios.

Sin embargo, escuchamos a uchos decir: Yo estoy al lado de Dios, doy mi servicio, me comunico, me alimento de su palabra. Pero tengo igulmente tribulaciones. Porque'?

Porque el mal se preocupa mas en molestar a quien esta de la mano de Dios, que a quien no lo esta'

El mal con sus representantes, sugieren el que no esta cerca de Dios, el que no sirve Dios, es quien no nos molesta. Pero aquel que sirve Dios y da' testimonio a diario ese ese si nos molesta. Ataquemos pues a ese que si molesta nuestro trabajo

ELEMENTOS PARA LIDERES CRISTIANOS

Cuando hablamos de lideres cristianos y lederazgo, hay siempre algunas preguntas quenos hacemos: Que es un lider?- Donde lo encontramos? – Por que' se necesiotan lideres?- Por que' seguimos al lider?- Por que' algunos desean convertirse en lideres?

Tanto su grupo como otras personas que lo conocen y estan familiarizados con su ministerio, esperan que la persona que inicio' una obra se un buen lider, ya sea laico, pastor, sacerdote o ministro bivocacional.

Cada iniciador de una iglesia neceita contester las preguntas indicadas arriba.

Hemos podido estudiar muchos tipos de lideres en la biblia.

Jesucristo es el lider modelo, pero tambien han existido muchos seres humanos a los Que Dios uso' como lideres, entre los favoritos estan: Noe', Abraham. Moises, Jose', Daniel y Pablo.

Cuando Dios puso en mi la inquietud de considerar el servicio cristiano, trate' de buscar un modelo dedicado a Dios y a los hombres.

Entonces, me pregunte': Que quiere Dios de mi como lider cristiano? y que debo hacer para ser un pastor efectivo?

Comence' a buscar y encontre' a Jose' en el Genesis41.33-41, sus hechos se amalgamaban formando un lider bueno y efectivo.

España fue durante muchos siglos atras un pais poderoso. Que dominaba los mares del mundo con su poderio naval. Pero esa Armada

Invencible fue derrotada dos veces, primero por los Britanos y luego por los Estados Unidos.

Que le falto' entonces a Espana asu Armada. Le falto' un barco Lider, una insignia de su poder.

Consideramos qu een todo grupo hay componentes para tener exito: Liderazgo, Organizacion, Moral y Planes.

El mas importante es el Liderazgo, porque hacia donde este va. Va toda la organizacion, va la moral de los seguidores y sus Planes.

El cauteverio en Babilonia desde 536 hasta 586 AJ

Los juduios desterrados se establecieron en Babilonia o bien se distribuyeron en colonias por la region del Tigris y del Eufrates.

La desgracia comun de Israel y de Juda' fue causa de que el nombre de judios se aplicase a los habitants de los dos reinos que hasta entonces habian estado separados y ahora compartian juntos los trabajos de destierro.

;Los judios vivian como esclavos y obreros trabajando en la construccionn de canales, jardines, palacios y otras obras serviles.

Su situacion civil fue en general tolerable, es mas algunos judios de las clases pudientes fueron tratados con distincion y llegaron como Daniel a ocupar puestos de importancia en el reino asirio.

La tentacion a la idolatria acarreo' riesgos a la religion, muchos judios que ya en su patria habian adorado idolos, sucumbieron del todo, en cambium otros muchos se purificaron en la cautividad.

En medio de la fastuosidad de la corte babilonica, deseaban a su tierra y al templo, por lo que sereunian como podian en sinagogas o en casas de familia donde oraban y leian las sagradas escrituras.

Dios les envio' profetas para que les instruyesenn y amonestasen e hiciesen saber a los paganos sobre la monumental obra de Dios.

Mas tarde Babilonia fue toınada sin resistencia por los persas y Ciro su rey nombro' virrey de la ciudad a Dario el medo.

Dario establecio por todo el reino 120 gobernadores bajo la dependencia de Daniel.

Envidiosos los magnates recabaron un decreto del rey que no se podia pedir cosa alguna o hacer cosa alguna sin el permiso del rey.

Esto lo hicieron con animo de hacer caer en desgracia a Daniel, pero este mas continuo' con sus oraciones a Dios, postrado en tierra y mirando hacia Jerusalem, fue por ello acusado y arrojado en castigo a la fosa de losleones. Dario no habia podido dormir esa noche pensando en Daniel y muy temprano se fue al, lago de los leones y con voz llorosa llamo' a Daniel. Al oir su respuesta el rey se llno' de jubilo, le ordeno' salir y a cambio ordeno' mandar a la fosa a los acusadores de Daniel, pero antes de que sus cuerpos llegasen a la fosa ya habian sido devorados por loos leones.

El rey en cambio proclamo' en todo el reino que se le temiera al Dios de Daniel.

Como dijimos Daniel tuvo una vida llena de actividades desafientes y ademas fue un gran profeta.

La liberacion de los judios 536 hasta el nacimiento de Cristo

Se dieron cuatro edictos a favor de los judios y despues de 70 anos de cautiverio.

Ciro publico' el primero poniendo fin al cautiverio. Dario les dio', permiso luego para seguir las obras del templo.

Hacia 458 **Artajerjes** envio' a sus aliado a rarregalar la situacion con Palestina y en 445 se los faculto' para reparar los muros de Jerusalem.

Conforme con las profecias, el rey Ciro ordeno' que todo miembro de la casa de Dios vaya a Jerusalem y edifique la casa de Dios.

Mas tarde se echaron las bases del nuevo templo, pero algunos judios se lamentaron porque este no tendria la pariencia ni la suntuasidad del de Salomon. Fue el profeta Ageo que los consolaba diciendo: Es cierto no tendra la misma suntuasidad de aquel, pero este sera' reconocido pues en el apareceria el Mesias.

Aqui aparece otro profeta Zacarias, quien Promete que el Mesias, aparecia en Jerusalem montado en un asno y que seria traicionado por 30 monedas.

Los judios gozaron de paz por unos 200 anos Se sumo' alrededor del sumosacerdote un consejo de ancianos o Sanhedrin quienes serian los encargados del sostenimiento de la ley y el orden religiosos.

Un hecho trascendente fue que en el 285 fue el haberse comenzado la version griega la Sagrada Escritura., se fueron traduiciendo todos los libros y por el 150 ya estaba la version completa del antiguo testamento.

Por el 200 los judios habin pasado a ser parte de los reyes de siria y descendientes de seleucidas general de Alejandro Magno.

Los otros siglos hasta el nacimiento del Mdesias no son muy conocidos en cuanto a la historia de los judios. Solo se conocen algunas narraciones de los macabeos que hablan de los fieles judios y de los impios y las luchas inyternas que esto provocaba.

Esta epoca no fue para nada fantastica en la vida del pueblo judio pero si una de las mas gloriasos porque muchos siguieron la voluntas de Dios.

Magnanimidad de un Lider

Davis al ser perseguido por Saul busca refugio en las montanas de Juda. Al saber esto Saul salio' en su persecucion con 3000 hombres, pero Dios puso en sus manos la vida del perseguidor al buscar este descanso en la misma cueva donde David estaba oculto.

David al ver al Rey y a sus hombres durmiendo se contento' solo con cortarle la orla del vestido.

Cuando el Rey salio' de la cueva. David lo sigue y le dice; Mi Rey y **Senor** y postrandose en tierra le dice; Porque Saul haces oidos a los que te dicen que yo estoy buscando tu mal? Sea juez Dios que ha puesto al Rey en mis manos; reconoce la orta de tu vestido que he cortado pero no extendere' mi mano contra ti! Al oir esto Saul le dijo: Mas justo eres tu que yo, que Dios te de' la recompense por lo que hoy has hecho conmigo y los dos se separaron en buena amistad.

Poco duro' en Saul ese buen proposito porque al poco tiempo salio' otra vez persiguiendo a David, cuando este lo supo se dirigio' al campamento del Rey donde **encontro'** a todos dormidos. Abisai' amigo de David quiso matar al Rey por lo que David le dijo: No lo mates! Quien extendera' su mano contra el ungido de Dios y sera' inocente? Toma la lanza real y la copa.

Ambos se fueron luego sin que nadie se diese cuenta, pues un sueno profundo de Dios habia venido sobre todos ellos y cuando ya se habian puesto a salvo en un cerro, David empezo' a gritar a Abner el general del Rey: Porque' no has guardado a tu Rey?

Despertandose tambien el Rey y dijo: No esta tu voz hijo mio David? y este respondio'

Soy Rey mio y **Senor** mio porque me persigues tanto, que mal he hecho contra ti?

Conocio' entonce Saul su injusticia y dijo: He pecado, vuelve David hijo mio y no te molestare mas, bandito seas hijo mio David! Pero David no confiandose se fue a la tierra de los filisteos.

Poco despues los filisteos reunieron un ejercito para luchar contra Israel, al saber esto Saul sale al encuentro y sento' su ejercito en los montes de Gilboa.

Un miedo terrible se apodero' de Saul por lo que consulto' a Dios pero no obtuvo respuesta, Entonces el Rey acude en su desesperacion a una maga para que le evocase a Samuel, entonces se le aparece este profeta anunciendole un desastroso fin y asi sucedio'.

Al dia seguiendo fueron derrotados losm israelitas y perecieron tres hijos del Rey y el mismo Saul viendose acosado por los flecheros, dijo a su escudero; desenvaina tu espada y matame, viendo Saul que su escudero no se atrevia a matar a su Rey, el mismo Saul tomo' la espada, la apoyo sobre su corazon y se dejo' caer sobre ella y murio'.

Davis es ungido Rey

Dijo Dios a Samuel. Llena tu cuerno de oleo y ve a Belen a la casa de Isai'.

Isa' salio' al encuentro de Samuel y le fue presentado a sus hijos.

Cuando se presento' el hijo mayor, dijo para si el profeta: Tal vez sea este el ungido de Dios, pero Dios le respondio' no mires su presencia o por su estatura, porque yo no juzgo por lo que parece.

Isai le fue presentado a otros de sus hijos, pero Samuel dijo: A ninguno d estos ha elegido Dios. No tienes otros hijos? pregunto' Samuel. TGengo al mas **pequeno** que ahora esta' apacentando las ovejas en el campo, su nombre es David.

Cuando llego' David, hermoso de rostro y cabellos rubios, dijo entonces Dios a Samuel este es el elgido, Samuel tomo' su cuerno de oleo y lo ungio' **en** medio de sus hermanos.

Saul que aun era Rey estaba enfermo. Los filisteos aprovecharon esto para emprender la guerra contra Israel. Habia entre los filisteos un gigante de nombre Goliat, el cual adelantandose ante los escuadrones israelitasles decia: Escoged entre vosotros a uno para combater conmigo, si este me mata seremos vuestros siervos, pero si yo le matare vosotros series nuestros esclavos. Y luego dijo: Hoy he insultado a los soldados de Israel y asi continuo' por 40 dias y **llos** israelitas se llenaron de miedo.

Es lider el que engendra miedo? No', lamas un lider verdadero engendra miedo.

Habia en el ejcrcito israelita tres hermanos de David, su padre quien queria saber sobre ellos mando' a Davis al campamento israelitra para saber como estaban.

Mientras hablaba con sus hermanos, Goliat empezo' a insultar a los israelitas. David entonces pregunto': Quien es ese filisteo que esta insultando al pueblo de Dios?

Dejadme que yo lo matare', sentencio' David.

Pero Saul, le dijo tu eres muy joven para batirte con el. Siendo yo pastor estrangule' leones que asaltaban el ganado de mim padre, respondio' David.

Saul le dijo, anda y que el **Senor** te **acompane**.

Cuando Goliat vio' a David se empezo' a reir y luego dijo: Soy acaso un perro para que vengas con un palo. Davis le respondio'; Tu vienes a mi con escudo, lanza y espada y yo voy a ti en nombre de Dios.

Viendo David que Goliat se acercaba furioso, tomo' una piedra y lanzandola con la honda esta se clavo' en**; la frente** de Goliat derribandolo a tierra, llego' hasta el David, tomo' su espada y le corto' la cabeza. Al ver esto los filisteos se echaron a huir.

Davis llevo' la cabeza de Goliat a Jerusalem y guardo' las armas del gigante en su casa.

Aqui podemos apreciar el caracter de lider en David. Porque fue decidido y audaz, No temio' a las fuerzas de los filisteosy a su gigante Goliat. Sintio' **en** todo momento la seguridad proveniente de Dios para lograr su cometido.

Los lideres pueden ser debiles fisicamente, pero gigantes de inteligencia y coraje.

La peste en Israel
La muerte de David

Otra dura prueba sobrevino sobre Israel por el orgullo de David.

Dios castiga la presuncion de David con una peste de **tres** dias que causo' la muetrte de 70.000 hombres.

Angustiado al extreme David suplico' a Dios diciendo: Yo soy el que he pecado, mis ovejas que han hecho? Vuelvasete ruego tu mano contra mi, Dios le envio' entonces al profeta Gad. diciendole que erigiere un altar para ofrecer sacrificios a Dios y asi lo hizo David y con esto se aplaco' el **Senor** y ceso' la, peste.

Treinta anos tenia Davis cuando comenzo' a reinar en Israel y goberno' por cuarenta.

Sintiendose viejo, convoco' a principes y grandes del reino y luego dijo a Salomon, su futuro heredero, conoce al Dios de tu padre y sirvele con corazon perfecto y Buena voluntad.

Le dice entonces a su hijo Salomon, defica el templo que Dios ha querido y el sera' contigo.

Sintiendose David cerca de su muerte volvio' a encomendar a Salomon la observancia de los mandamientos divinos.

Davis **fue** enterrado en la ciudad de David, donde fueron sepultados casi todos los reyes de Israel.

David aparece en casi todos los detalles de su vida como figura lider y tipo de Jesucristo.

David supo reunir en su persona las tres grandes figuras de Jesucristo, fue Rey y Rey **segun** el corazon de Dios, fue Profeta en sus Salmos y ejercioo' hasta cierto punto la function sacerdotal.

Podemos decir que David ante estas circunstancias, fue un luchador, un lider y un hombre que con magnanimidad supo servir a Dios y a los hombres.

Supo buscar una negociacion con Saul para unirse a el y permancer intacto a los ojos de Dios.

David fue una figura de liderazgo,.

SALOMON REY Y LIDER DE ISRAEL

Apenas veinte anos tenia Salomon cuando subio' al trono y sus primeras disposiciones fueron cum[plir con los encargos de David.

Salomon amo' a Dios y cumplio' con sus preceptos y fue a Gabaon a ofrecer sacrificios al **Senor**.

Apareciose Dios en sus **suenos** y le dijo; Pide lo que quieras y yo te lo dare'.

Salomon le responde: Tu **Senor** mio hiciste Rey a tu siervo, mas ypo soy un nino debil e inexperto, da' a tu siervo uncorazon docil para que sepa hacer justicia y dicernir entre lo bueno y lo malo.

Agrado' esto a Dios y le respondio'; Por cuanto no has pedido vida larga, ni riquezas nil as almas de tus enemigos, sino solo sabiduria para hacer justicia, yo te dare' sabiduria e inteligencia que ninguno antes ha tenido, tambien te dare' riquezas y Gloria y si guardaras mis mandamietos tambien te dare' una larga vida.

Uan de las primeras cosas que hizo Salomon fue construer el templo de Jerusalem sobre el monte Moriah.

Salomon renovo' su amistad con Hiram Rey de Tiro, hjizo un tratado con el sobre los materiales en operarios que necesitaria.

El Rey de Tiro se comprometio' a enviarle. Madera de pino y cedro y piedras preciosas.

A cambio de esto Salomon enviaria cebada, trigo, aceite y vino.

Salomon eligio' 30.000 obreros de todo Israel.

A los cuatro anos de su reinado Salomon comenzo' la construccion del templo, al cual dio' en lineas generales la semejanza del tabernaculo.

El interior del templo estaba dividido en dos partes, el santo y el santo de los santos.

Dentro del templo todo era de oro y piedras preciosas y todo todo el mobiliario tambien era de oro y marmol.

Al cabo de 7 anos termino Salomon el templo.

Salomon construyo' tambien un palacio magnifico, el trono era de oro con incrustaciones de marfil.

Embellecio' tambien Salomon a todo Israel y especialmente a Jerusalem y los pueblos y Reyes vecinos mostraron su admiracion por Salomon enviandole hermosos regalos.

Pero, el brillo de **tanta** grandeza deslumbro' a Salomon y contra la voluntad de Dios tomo' para si mujres paganas que le pervirtieron a tal punto de edificar templos para los idolos.

Salomon fue por su nombre por el splendor, la riqueza y la paz durante su reinado.

Fue conocido por su sabiduaria y justicia es figura de Jesucristo.

Enojado el **Senor** con Salomon le dijo: Ya no has guardado mis mandamientos dividire' tu reino y lo dare' a un siervo tuyo.

LOS PROFETEAS LIDERES COMO ELEMENTO DE CAMBIO

El reino de Juda'

El reino de Juda' recibio' este nombre porque la tribu de Juda' era la mas importante. Todos sus reyes descendian de la decada real de David, fueron reyes legitimos, por mas que pocos de ellos guardaron la ley de Dios.

Su capital fue Jerusalem donde estaba el templo edificado por Salomon. Por lo cual se conservo' mejor la fe' en el Dios unico. A pesar de todo esto algunos reyes introdujeron la idolatria en el reino.

Roboan, hijo de Salomon fue el que introdujo dioses falsos, pero su nieto Asa' hizo lo que era bueno para la voluntad de Dios. Derribo' estatuas a los falsos dioses, quebro' los alares erigidos a esos falsis dioses y talo' bosques que estaban preparados para esas falsas divinidades.

Los profetas de Juda':

De todos los profestas que aparecieron en Juda', Isaias fue el mas grande de todos, predico' por mas de medio siglo hasta.

Este profeta se hizo famoso, por reprender las supersticiones, inmoralidades e idolatries de los judios y al mismo tiempo anuncio' los terriblesd castigos sobre ste pueblo infiel.

Los reyes de Siria e Israel se aliaron contra Juda'. Luego los asirios, babilonios, egipcios y de Tiro se lanzaron sobre Juda'.

Isaias es el primero en anunciar la llegada de un Mesias.

Tambien anuncio' Isaias quie ese Mesias naceria de una virgen y que su nombre seria Emmanuel.

Tambien Isaias anuncia su pa.sion y muerte para salvar al mundo.

EZEQUIEL, UN PROFETA LIDER

Entre los profetas Ezequiel el profeta de la divina fidelidad. El Eclesiastes 49:10,11. hace de Ezequiel un bello elogio.

Durante 27 anos ejercio' su vision profetica entre los cautivos y contra los falsos profetas.

El fin del cautiverio **en** Babilonia, asi como la llegada del Mesias esta perfectamente descripto por Ezequiel bajo la figura de la resurreccion de los muertios.

Fue llevado el profeta en espiritu a un gran campo cubierto de huesios humanos, por orden d Dios mando' Ezequiel a que los huesos se levantasen y se irguieron al instante y se uniron a otros huesos, cubiriendose de **nervios** y se unio' a ellos el espiritu, pusieronse de pie y comenzaron a vivir.

Ezequiel se presenta como la figura lider de la divina fidelidad Dios.

Dijole Dios a Ezequiel; Todos estos huesos representan la figura be Israel, he aqui pueblo **mio dice Ezequiel que yo os sacare' de vuestros sepulcros y los conducire' a la tierra de Israel.**

EL PROFETA DANIEL

Se ha dicho que Daniel es uno de los mas grandes aparecidos en los **ultimos** siglos de la Antigua alianza.

Su sabiduria e inteligencia le hicieron igualmnete famoso.

Daniel al escribir se propuso conserver la fe de los judios, no solo durante el destierro, sino tambien durante la era de las persecuciones.

Daniel nos habla de el reino de Dios. Daniel es una de las pruebas mas evidentes **en** favor de la verdad de la religion revelada.

Ezequiel alaba muchas veces como contemporano de Dniel y le compara con **Noe** y con Job en la santidad.

Daniel salva a Susana

Vivia en Babilonia un joven distinguido de nioembre Joaquin y tenia por esposda a una mujer muy Hermosa llamada Susana.

En su casa solian reunirse judios y entre ellos dos viejos deignados juices para impartir justicia entre le pueblo.

Cierto dia, al verla sola a Susana se escondieron en sui jardin y le dijeronL Si no quieres que te acusemos de adulteria debes hacer lo que nosostros queremos contigo. Susana se niega a los bajos deseos de los dos viejos.

Pero Daniel ilumidado por Dios le envia al juicio en contra e Susana y le dice a los dos viejos dime: Donde las has visto pecando a Susana la he visto debajo de un lentisco y separadamente llama al otro viejo y le pregunta: Donde has visto pecando a Susana y el viejo exclama debajo de un ciruelo. Los dos mientes dijo Daniel. Ninguno e Uds coincide **con las acusaciones contra esta mujer.**

Convencios los dos viejos que habian levantado una calumnia contra Susana, fueron apedreados conforme a la ley.

A Daniel se lo ve' como un gran profeta no solom por la interpretacion que el hace sobre Dios, sino por ser el quien logra que la religion era el camino para la esperanza.

Daniel fue quien sirvio' ante Nabucodonosor y este lo eligio' en su corte.

DECADENCIA DE ISRAEL Y LOS PROFETAS

No hay duda que con la muerte de Salomon, comienza la decadencia del pueblo de Israel.

Ese reino duro' 201 anos y tuvo 19 reyes.

El otro reino el de Juda' subsistio' 343 anos bajo el gobierno de 20 reyes.

Ambos reinos, fueron infieles a Dios y estuvieron con frecuencia en guerra el uno contra el otro. Durante ese periodo Dios suscito varones santos llamados Profetas, para recorder a los pueblos los preceptos de la, ley divina y de un modo especial para anunciar la venida de un Redentor.

Los profetas no eran lideres pero aconsejaban a los reyes la orientacion a seguir en los gobiernos.

A la muerte de Salomon su hijo de nombre Roboan se hizo proclamar rey

La asamblea le dijo al nuevo rey: Tu padre nos ha impuesto un yugo muy pesado de impuestos, hazlo mas suave y te serviremos.

No le gusto; esto al rey y pidio el consejo a los ancianos, quienes le dijeron. Hablales con dulzura y respeto y aydalos en lo que te piden, tampoco le agrado' esto al rey y entonces pidio' el consejo a los jovenes, quienes le dijeron: Sit u padre le ha puesto unyugo muy pesado yo les hatre' mas pesado, si mi padre azoto' con latigo, yo os azotare' con hierro.

Cuando el rey le comunico' esto al pueb;lo se sublevaron las diez tribus de Israel.

Roboan se marcho' a Jerusalem y reunio' un gran ejercito para someter a los rebeldes, entonces la voz de Dios le dijo: No salgais de campana ni peleis con vuestros hermanos, vuelvase cada cual a su casa porque yo soy el que lo ha dispuesto.

Por lo visto Raboam no era un lider a quienes todos seguian, fue un rey a quien algunos le servian, pero como empleados en una empresa se sublevaron a su jefe cuando este hablo' de azote y mas yugo.

GRANDEZA DEL MISTERIO DE LA ENCARNACION

El misterio de la Encarnacion sobrepasa el modo de entender humano.

Es un ineffable portento nuevo, un prodigio inaudito, adorado de los Angeles y predicado a las naciones, y recibido en la Gloria como dice San Pablo.

Nos revelo la grandeza inmensa de un Dios y su amor que para redimir al mundo se anonado hasta tomar la forma de siervo y habitar en el mundo.

La importancia historica de este hecho marca epoca en la historia de la humanidad ty poe supuesto en los formadores de nuevos lideres para continuar esta obra misteriosa y divina.

Jususcristo se encarno' para salvar al mundo, porque el pecado les habia privado de la gracia y ademas les habia echo esclavos del demonio y del infierno.

Jesus es Dios y es hombre, y como hombre y en el padecio' y murio' la naturaleza humana.

Jesus creo' el camino para otros lideres llamados y elegidos siguieran su obra en la tierra.

Define la redencion; La redencion es un misterio en el que el hijo de Dios, hecho hombre ha tomado nuestras inquidades y muriendo en la cruz a satisfecho por nosotros a la justicia divina.

Tremenda carga para Dios enviar a su propio hijo a morir para salvar al mundo del pecado.

Todo lo podemos ver en la vida publica de Jesus y su aparacion trazada por los cuatro evangelistas.

EL MESIANISMO Y PRINCIPALES FIGURAS

Se designa con el nombre de mesianismo todo el conjunto de doctrinas, creencias, y esperanzas relativas.

1- El reino de Dios que debe establecerse sobre la tierra
2- A la persona y mision del Mesias que sera' el repersentante de Dios
3- A los destinos del pueblo de Israel

Estos ideales mesianicos, que tiene origen en la primera promesa del redentor, se van aclarando y haciendose mas vivos en el pueblo de Israel a medida que este pueblo especialmente elegido por Dios, recibe de sus profetas nuevas revelaciones acerca de las personas y la mision del Mesias.

En un resumen de lo que llevamos apuntado en el Antiguo Testamento se han senalado las personas que fueron figura. Vease a lo dicho sobre Abraham, Isaac, Jose', Moises, David, y Salomon.

Como pudimos decir antes, fueron figuras previstas por la redencion, actuaron como modelo cada uno de ellos en diferentes pero parecidas circunstancias. Fueron lideres en su pueblo, algunos gobernaron y fueron reconocidos por otros pueblos tambien, como ocurre en la figura de un lider, el lider es reconocido por la mayoria.

LIDERES EN EL NUEVO TESTAMENTO

Al principio antes que el mundo fuese, ya existia el hijo de Dios, que debia hacerse hombre y que tambien se llama verbo o palabra.

Por medio de la palabra nosotros damos a conocer nuestros pensamientos. Y a Jusucristo el Hijo de Dios se llama Verbo porque Dios se nos da' a conocer por medio de El.

Ya que por medio del Verbo, Dios hizo todo cuanto existe en el mundo, y por el dio' la vida a todo lo que vive.

Y esto es porque el Verbo era la vida y esta vida fue la luz de los hombres. Y esta luz vno a brillar en las tinieblas del muindo. Pero asi como a la salida bdel sol, precede la aurora, asi tambien antes de aparcer Jesus en este mundo se manifiest Juan el cual con el resplandor se su predicacion hizo volver las miradas a Jusus.

Juan fue un lider, el no era la luz simo un reflejo anunciador de la verdadera Luz.

Y aparecio' la Luz, el verbo se hizo carne y habito' enttre nosotros.

En los evangelios tenemos la verdadera fuente para conocer la vida de Jesus.

Precisamente la palabra evangelio significa Buena nueva o sea toda Buena noticia.

Para el profeta Ezequiel y al princpioio de sus vaticinios, nos describe la Gloria de Dios con la imagen de una nube de fuego que se mueve tirade por una cuadtriga de seres misteriosos. Tiene cada uno cuatro aspectos.

La tradicion cristiana ha querido ver en estos animals los simbolos de los cuatro evangelios., que difunden el nombre gloriosm de Jesus.

San Mateo escribio' el primer evangelio en la lengua que se hablaba en Palestina que era el arameo o el sirio-caldeo, pronto se hizo una traduccion griega y el arameo quedo' olvidado.

San Marcos, compuso el Segundo evangelio en griego para uso de los convertidos del paganismo, hacia los anos 60 mientras estaba en Roma.

San Lucas, escribio' tambien en griego durante la primera prision de San Pablo en Roma.

San Juan discipulo amado de Jesus, escribio' en griego el cuarto evangelio en Efeso. San Juan escribio' en palabras que siempre repetia. "Estas cosas han sido escritas para creais que Jususn es el hijo de Dios y para que creyendo tengais vida en su nombre"

Los evangelios son dignos de fe porque fueron inspirados por el Espiritu Santo, y son autenticos, y veraces.

Su autenticidad proviene porque fueron escritos por los autores a quienes se les atribuye.

Se conservan mas de 2300 copias en pergamino original.

Ellos fueron testigos de lo que vieron, son competentes y no se enganan.

Ademas los hechos que ellos refieren sucedieron a la vista de todos.

Los autores de los evamgeliosm fueron personas sencillas que dan cita de todo lo que vieron y dan pormenores de sitios y testigos.

No hay razon alguna para pensar que estuvieran mintiendo.

Los evangelistas como lieres naturals y sencillos arcaron una epoca, la dejaron grabada con sus palabras y sus hechos.

Esa epoca no tiene fin, sus libros lideran otros libros de hombres que como ellos han escrito sobre la vida de Jesus.

Podemos dar una interpretacion diciendo que cada uno de ellos con sus tendencias escribio' y a ellos les siguieron millones y millones que hasta hoy comparten sus evangelios. Por eso decimos que Mateo, Lucas, Juan y Marcos son lideres naturales.

El lider Productivo

Como en empresas y administraciones de paises. El lider debe generar y producir.

Como definimos a un gerente de empresa: Como aquel profesional que valiendose de los elementos que posee es capaz de generar mas negocios productivos para el bien de su empresa, de sus empleado y para su propio bien.

El mismo ejemplo aplica para un pais o una corporacion.

No importa cuan ese gerente dea de ordenado en sus papeles y cuan bien cuide la administracion de su negocio, mas que eso debe saber generar mas oportunidades para crecer.

Lo mismo ocurre con la fe de cada uno. Debemos dejarla producir, ampliarla, llegar mas gente, que mas almas nos conprendan el camino elegido.

Podemos tener muy buenos corazones y ser muy amantes de la verdad y de; la justicia, pero mas que eso debemos hacer producir mas seres que amen a Dios.

Tambien mas adeptos para su iglesia.

Los libros dicen y con cierta dureza, que, aquel gerente que siendo un gran administrador y una Buena persona, no sabe generar nuevos **negoci0os** y oportunidades para su empresa no puede estar en ese puesto.

Los libros de gerenciamineto muestran al gerente como elemento de cambio, como a un creador nato y un ser imaginativo, lo mismo ocurre con el hombre de Dios

Juan el bautista.
Otro ejemplo y precursor de Jesus

Porque mencionamos al bautista y le damos una especial atencion, porque el fue el precursor del Mesias.

Hacia el ano 26 Juan el bautista, vino predicando penitencia y bautizando por toda la region del Jordan

A todos decia; Preparad el camino para el Mesias, haced penitencia y enderezad sus sendas, porque el reino de los cielos se acerca.

El bautismo era una ceremionia simbolica y figurative, simbolizaba la purificacion y representaba el bautismo de Cristo.

La impresion causada por Juan que se vestia con piel de camello y que no tenia otro alimento mas que miel y langostas silvestres, fue enorme en todas las clases del pueblo.

Una muchedumbre le aclamaba y se acercaba a recibir el bautismo.

Su vida austere, vigorosa y de caracter y con audacia se imponia a todos.

Juan reprendia y castigaba el orgullo y la hipocresia, pedia que los soldados fuesen justos y les pedia honestidad a los hombres publicos.

Juan se mostraba como un verdadero lider, era audaz, inquieto y de fuerte personalidad.

Jesus habia dejado Nazaret y se encamino' al Jordan donde tambien fue bautizado por Juan.

Por un tiempo, muchos creyeros que Juan era el Mesias, pero el siempre decia, yo solo bautizo, pero vendra' otro mas fuerte que yo, de quien no soy digno de desatar ni la correa de sus zapatos!

Porque Juan? Le dedicamos esta hoja a Juan. Porque en el miramos a un inspirador y a un precursor. Un lider es un precursor como Juan, y como Juan un lider es inpirador. Tiene caracter y es audaz.

Perseverante en la oracion. La perseverancia del lider.

Asi como se es perseverante en muchos aspectos de la vida, tambien el lider es perseverante en la oracion.

Jesus dijo: Quien de vosotros si tuvieses un amigo y fueses a el en el medio de la noche a decirle: Amigo prestame tres panes, porque acaba de llegar un amigo de viaje y no tengo que ponerle delante.

Y el otro respondieses: No me seas molesto, porque ya esta' **cerrada** la puerta y tanto mis criados como yo estamos durmiendo, no puedo dartelos.!!

Pero, si el otro persevarante llamando a la puerta, os digo, que cuando no se levantare ante su amigo, cierto por su inoportunidad se levantara' y le dara' ciuantos panes hubiese menester.

Y yo os digo: Pedid y se os dara', buscad y encontraras, llamad y se os abrira', porque todo aquel que pide **recibe**, todo aquel que busca halla, todo aquel que llama' se le abrira'.

Muchas veces se recurre a la perseverancia para obtener un cometido.

Acasso un hijo que pide al padre pan, este la da' piedra, o si puede huevos se le da' una serpientre o si pide pez se le da' un escorpion.

Cuanto mas el padre celestial puede dar a sus hijos.

El lider es perseverante, no se ensalza. El que se ensalza puede ser humillado, pero aquel que se humilla puede ser ensalzado.

El lider nunca se ensalza, los demas tal vez lo hagan con el.

El lider conoce su espacio y lo hace muy **pequeno** para que sus ovejas tengan mas lugar para corer y saltar.

En una empresa, los empleado pide espacio para demostrar lo utiles que pueden ser para esa empresa y el lider valiendose de su capacidad se los da'.

El lider quiere el progreso de sus empleados dandole espacio para desenvolverse.

El lider no es egoista, tampoco es envidioso.

El lider genuino, habla con sabiduria e inteligencia, no se preocupa por las criticas.

Es mas facil ser jefe que lider, por supuesto ser jefe es una posicion para mandar y demostrar muchas veces para que esta' uno que manda, pero el lider conduce, guia, conoce muy bien a cada uno de su manada.

Ayuda al debil, iniciando una tarea conjunta. El lider insiste muchas veces antes de tomar una decision sobre alguien que no le devuelve de la misma manera.

En la vida cotidiana, **en** la vida de negocios y el la vida de la fe', el lider es **unico**, da' demostracion con su perseveracion y su humildad.

Las perpectivas para los nuevos lideres

La voz lider es **realmnete** algo nueva en el, idioma. Proviene del ingles leader.

Relativamente hace poco tiempo que se ha empezado a usar en el lenguaje corriente, hoy hablamos de lideres de naciones, lideres de empresas, lideres religiosos, lidres de grupos, **deportistas** lideres, y tambien lo asiciamos marcas y productos lideres o servicios lideres.

Lo asociamos a la idea de lo mejor en **forma** inmediata.

Si decimos quien fabrica un producto cuaklquiera y es una marca reconocido y ese producto tiene los mejores ingrdientes, buen precio o precio competitivo y esta tan bien distribuido que en la ciudad que estemos lo encontramos, decimo que es un producto y marca lider.

De la misma manera a los hombres y mujeres lideres pensamos que estan donde stan porque son los mejores.

La mejoropcion para una nacion, una empresa o un grupo.

En los grupos deoracion ocurre lo mismo hay un lider que guia la lectura y la discusion final y las conclusions.

Los lideres son elegidos por su grupo, los lideres religiosos en el cristianiosmo se considera son elegido por hombres pero con la ayuda de la mano de Dios.

Son los mejores, en todo.

No basta con saber mucho o ser inteligente, se debe ser el mejor en forma completa, dando el ejemplo con cada servicio.

El que no vive para servir no sirve para vivir, dijo cierta vez un pensador **hindu'**.

Seamos sercvidores dando testimonio en cada acto del nuestro dia y agradezcamos A Dios por haberle, poder servido ese dia y pedir por otro dia.

El lider y sus luchas diarias

Que vale mas aquel que da' de lo que le falta o aquel que da' de lo que le sobra /

La respuesta parece muy clave, siempre tiene mas valor el que entrega de lo que le falta, mas de quien entrega lo que le sobra.

El que entrega de lo que le falta o esta con necesidad tiene un valor infinito y grande a los ojos de Dios.

Mas el que entrega de lo que le sobra, si bien es una Buena accion, no lo es como el que sufre por arreglarselas con menos de lo poco que tenia.

Es un servidor para Dios y para los hombres.

El lider tiene batallas contantes.

Aquel que convive con Dios puede ser mas aracado por el mal que aquel que no convive **en la fe de Dios.**

Porque?

Porque el mal ataca mas al que lo molesta que a quien no oo molesta.

Es muy sencillo de comprender.

Del mas tiene seguidores, algunos porque realmente proceden con maldad y otros son seguidores virtuales porque no molestan al que hace mal, tampoco lo condenan.

El hombre de Dios libra batallas todo el tiempo con el mal.

Muchos preguntas a quienes son fieles Dios.

Pero, tu que eres un hombre de Dios, un hombre probado y justo. Con una grandeza de corazon infiniota que defiendes la verdad y la justicia, porque a te viene tantas tribulaciones?

Tambien parece simple de aclarar. Porque con esa actitud positive hacia Dios estoy en cada acto mplestando al mal.

Aquel que no lucha por Cristo, el que no se preocupa por cuantos perjudican al mundo no es tan molestado.

Pero aquel que si libra batallas todo el tiempo, ese es constantemente molestado, muchas veces las tribulacions le **vienen** a el o se le demuestran con otros miembros de su familia.

Las tribulaciones para los justos, son la guerra constante declarada al mal.

En las luchas diarias encontramos que hacer

Cuando alguien de nuestro entorno nos miente, que de ese no lo esperabamos estamos ante una tribulacion puesta por el mal.

Cuando se nos complica la Buena comunicacion con cualquier miembro de nuestro entorno familiar o no lo entendemos ahi tambien hay una demostracion de que el mash ace la confusion.

El mal hace no es un elemento de cambio. El Lider como elemento de cam, bio lo vence.

Los lideres vencen batallas todos los dias, el mal no da' tregua.
Un conflicto en el mundo entre dos naciones que no se entienden es porque el mal no los deja hacaerse entender y eso lo transmite a traves de los hombres.
El mal se vale de los hombres para demostrar lo que quiere.
Los hombres hablamos por el mal muchas veces.

Entonces, que hace el lider de la fe'
Jamas se doblega, sabra' que otro dia lo sorprendera' con un problema no deseado.

El lider vence.

Para los lideres e hoy, con tantos conflictos individuales y mundiales, Dios es la **unica** respuesta para llegar a encontrar soluciones.

Muchas veces decimos cuando estab mas cerca de DIOS tenia problemas por supuesto, pero cunado nos alejamos de Dios los problemas se multiplicand mas y mas.

Cual es el camino?

El camino es la oracion. La oracion es la comunicacion y el dialogo con Dios.

Dios nos responde siempre, solo debemos interpretarlo.

Dios no habla muchas veces a traves de nuestros hijos, nos habla con una idea en nuestra mente, Dios nos habla por medio de la lectura

Hay un formula entices?

No hay formulas exactas, el, poder de la oracion es tan grande que supera lo conocido Hagamos lo possible para estar cerca de Dios y el hara' lo imposible con nosostros.

EL LIDER REFORMADOR

Martin Lutero fue sin duda un reformador, con una figura pragmatica dio' la movilidad al protestantismo.

Para Lutero la **unica** autoridad y fuente de sabiduria es la Biblia.

Y menciona un criterio muy abierto de enetender como en muchas religions. La **unica** manera de acceder al padre celestial es mediante Jesus.

La teologia para Lutero tenia y tiene entre los seguidores de la Iglesia Luterana y con practices diferentes a los de la Iglesia Catolica Romana.

Lutero fue un ejemplo de lider reformador, contra el surgio' la contrareforma, sin embargo hoys us seguidores y despues de mas de 500 anos lo ven como un Lider nato.

Lutero comienza adiscutir el tema de las indulgencias que se otorgaban a las personas.

Para la Iglesia Catolica se otorgaban indulgencia con la oracion y pero tambien y en otroas casos parecia que se llegaba a comercializar la obtencion de indulgencias.

La fe y su poder, el amor a cristo y su infinito perdon no se compran.

Las indulgencias son y fueron una manera de que se condenen los pecados a cambio de mayor acercamiento a Dios.

La oracion y la penitencia, mas la comulgacion con Dios y el pedir perdon por las malas obras eran fundamentalemnte el camino de obtener el perdon por las indulgencias.

Pareciera que para otros se hizo una materializacion de la indulgencia.

Las **indiulgencia** se vendian como un material o un epacio fisico.

Las obras de Dios nom se omercializan de **ningun** modo.

Lutero fue un lider que comulgo' con Dios, que lucho' ante los traficantes de la fe' y dio' como **unico** camino la fe' y la verdad **en** Dristo.

Hoy muchos aun crean que entregando dinero para obras es el camino positive para obtener el reino de los cielos y en parte esto es cieerto.

Pero, podemos entregar dinero a la **comun** idad que es un acto fantastico, pero lo dbemos hacer con el corazon abierto y siempre pensando que es un servicio a Dios.

No podemos pecar y entonces hacer una **buerna** obra. Es un facilismo tactico decir, peco despues me arrepiento y doy una ayuda y Dios m,e perdona.

Ese no es el camino correcto, lo correcto es no volver a pecar y si volver a hacer buenas obras.

LA ELECCION DE
LOS DOCE APOSTOLES
LA ELECCION DE
FORMAR LIDERES

Cuando Jesus volvio' a Galilea, las gentes lo seguian para oirlo y curarse de sus dolencias.

Un dia Jesus despues de pasar la noche orando, llamo' a sus discipulos a un monte y eligio' a 12 de entre ellos.

Los llamo' Apostoles es decir Enviados.

Estos fueron Pedro, el primero, Pedro es roca, es fortaleza. Como un futuro lider de su gran empresaJesus eligio' a alguien fuerte de espiritu y de caracter. Con una gran fuerza y Personalidad, pero con un corazon grande y tierno.

Sobre la roca edifico' su Iglesia.

Edificaer sobre roca no sobre arena, al igual que nuestra fe'. Si edificamos sobre arena al subir la marea esa construccion desparece. Pero si edificamos sobre roca esta estara' alli siempre.

Los lideres deja huella. Pedro dejo' una huella para ser vista y multiplicada.

En Pedro vemos a un lider gigante, fuerte, inquebrantable con decision y personalidad definida. Como hombre de accion y de gran vida interior.

El lider deja huella, marca un camino. Deciamos que no seamos como la saves que Cruzan el sielo sin dejar huella, o como los bascos en el mar quie su huella desaparece casi al instante de haber pasado.

Hay una anecdota que lei cierta vez en un libro sobre gerenciamiento de empresas.

Habia en Inglaterra un Primer Ministro muy joven, con 33 anos llego' a ser Jefe de Gobierno, su apellido era Pitt.

Un dia Pitt muere y va a golpear a las puertas del Reino de losd Cielos.

Lo recibe San Pedro y le dice: Que raro un politico por aqui?

Y Pitt responde, pero Pedro yo no hice nada, no **perjudique** a nadir, ni a mi familia ni a mi pueblo. No fue corrupto, no abandone' a misd hijos, No hice nada.

Pedro le responde: No me digas lo que no has hecho, dime que hiciste.

Lo mismo que a Pitt, a los lideres se les pide cuentas de las acciones que hicieron, que progreso cumplieron, cuantos hospitals crearon, En cuanto mejoraron los beneficios para el ciudadano o empleado de una empresa

No lo que no hiecieron por temor.

Nos poemos equivocar de Buena fe' y eso no es grave. El que trabaja duro se puede equivocar muchas veces, no solmos **infallibles.**

Pero el que no hace nada, no puede equivocarse, pore so de no hacer nada.

La leyenda de Pedro y Pitt es simbolica. Para medir cuanto hemos hecho bien y cuanto mal.

JESUS EL LIDER, DIOS Y HOMBRE VERDADERO, SU PERSONA DIVINA Y SUS DOS NATURALEZAS

Jesus es hijo de Dios completo en su divinidad y completo en su humanidad.

Compuesto tambien de un alma dotada de razon, semejante en todo a anosotros con la exepcion del pecado, engendrado por el padre antes de los siglos por su divinidad, nacido de la virgen Maria, dos naturalezas, la divina y la humana.

Tambien hay dos enttendimientos uno divino en cuanto a Dios y uno humano en cuanto al hombre.

El jesucristo hombre habito' entre nosostros, como cualquier otro hombre, sin abandoner su naturaleza divina, eligio' nacer y morir como cualquiera mas aun entre la pobreza. Es la parte mas grandiose de un lider universal, la humilded dentro de su grandiosidad. Es que la humildad es la marca por escelencia de los grandes.

En Jesucristo no hay dos personas, pero si dos naturalezas. Jesucristo es una sola persona y es la divina.

Es btambien la segunda persona de la santisima Trinidad.

San Patricio acostumbraba a valerse de un trebol de **tres** hojas para explicar la santisima Trinidad,: Tres personas distintasn y un Dios verdadero, tres hojas igualesl tiene el trebol y un solo tallo que las une y las alimenta.

Asi como por se tallo se alimentan las hojas, y por sus marcadas corre la savia de vida, asi nosostros nos alimentamos de la palabra de Dios.

El trebol es un ejemplo perfecto de tres hojas que nacen y se nutren de la misma nanera, No hay diferencias, el color, la textura, los dettalles de cada una son iguales, la nutirente es la misma, pero un solo tallo del cual se formaron.

La naturaleza divina del padre y la demostracion del ser humano para que confien en el, muchos dicen muchas veces, Jesus podria **haber** nacido en un gran palacio, cubieerto de oro yu piedras preciosas, con muchos sirvientes, porque **entoncs** eligio un **pequeno** establo en las montanas?

Lideres contemporaneos

Llamamos lideres contemporaneos a aquellos lideres que estan en el presente y son futuras matrices para formar mas lideres que seran historia dentro de mucho tiempo.

Los lideres contemporaneos habitan entre nosotros, cuando mencionamos el lider del ingles leader pensamos en alguien que con mucha integridad se ha mostrado genuine ante los demas y ha sabido ganar un lugar entre otros.

El lider tiene autoridad pero no es autoritario.
El autoritario quiere demostrar poder porque lo tiene pero esinseguro sin no se demuestra con esa peculiaridad.
El lider genuine no es autoritario, sabe escuchaer es flexible y comparte con su equipo sus ideas y las ideas de los emas.
Por eso decimos que los que tienen autoridad y lo viven diciendo son realmente temerosos por perderla e inseguros de ellos mismos.

Podemos mencionar muchos lideres contemporaneos pero algunos posiblemente sean verdaderos lideres.

Que ocurre con los lideres de las iglesias en el mundo.
En las naciones de la tierra.
En las empresa y corporaciones.
Los hombres de negocios, los maestros, los que instruyen a otros Seran todos lideres?

Muchas veces escuchamos que los lideres mundiales se reunen en una ciudad para trar el cambio climatico o que esos mismos lideres de las naciones mas poderosas tieien en sus manos el futuro economico y tecnologico del mundo.

En algun momento fueron elegidos por las mayorias, pero alcabo de un tiempo esas mayorias disminuyeron cambiaron de posicion y esa mayoria fue equiparada por otros que eran minoria.

Que ocurrio'? que el lider reconocido perdio' su poder y perdio' su liderazgo, sin ambargo decimos y lo seguimos llamado lider.

El lider no nace se hace

Eso es muy cierto el lider de hoy se hace, se nutre de su capacidad para guiar por el mejor camino pero no nacio' lider. [ara muchas personas los lideres nacen y eso no es asi.

El lider completo

El lider complete es aquel lider que valiendose del poder que le dieron otros al reconocerlo como el mejor y como el pilar indispensable de su equipo.

Grupo. Empresa o nacion.

Es el lider indiscutido, no caen sobre el otros que no fueron elegidos pero que conocer y pueden guiar mejor que el.

Por eso el lider sale de su manada de su equipo.

El lider complete, es aquel que sabiendo transmitir la palabra, elabora un plan para su grey, y conduce interpretando el sentir de su equipo.

En una empresa privada, podemos decir que es parecido. Aque; que conduce una empresa, que interpreta a su gente y le da' un tono cristiano a sus decisions va a ser doblelente valorado, no solo por su empresa sino poer las empresas de la competencia.

El lider no destruye, a otros para ganar una posicion, el lider da' a conocer que su plan es mas conveniente, tampoco dece que es el mejor.

El lider respeta a los demas como los demas lo respetan a el.

No sabe de rencores ni odios es tal cual es con una vision cristiana por sobre todas las cosas.

CONTINUIDAD HISTORICA DE JESUCRISTO, UN LIDER Y SU VIDA SE PROLONGA EN LA IGLESIA

La obra del lider, estaba cumplida, redimido el hombre, fundada la Iglesia y abiertas las puertas del cielo

La semilla del evangelio quedaba escondida en la tierra y pronto empoezaria a germinar: la venida del espritu santo en el dia de pentecostes, bajo lenguas de fuego; las numerosas conversaciones primero de judios y luego de gentiles., la actuacion de San Pedro como primer vicario de Cristo, la dispersion de los apostolos por el mundo, los viajes de San Pablo, luego las persecuciones, los martirios, las victories. Un mundo convertido. El germen milagroso que se desarrolla siglo tras siglo en la jerarquia, en las doctrinas, en las almas, y en las sociedades a pesar de las oposiciones, de las amenazas y de las luchas mas encarnizadas.

A la historia conmovedora de los lideres iniciadores, los lideres inspiradores, los lideres inductors, y la vida de Jesus el fenomeno religioso mas grande de la humanidad, suce otra; la historia de la iglesia, de la sociedad divina por el fundada, por el asistida y protegida.

Con la parte final del nuevo testamento, tenemos los hechos de los apostoles: Las 14 epistolas de San Pablo, el apocalipsis de San Juan el evangelista, 2 de San Pedro y 3 de San Juan.

Escritos lideres que mantienen y mantendran vigencia por siempre.

Los apostololes tuvieron una actividad misional, pero por sobre ello la predicacion del nombre de Jesuscristo.

Todo esto forma y conforma la historia de la iglesia, y como **segun** el plan de Jesusel espiritu santo descendio', sobre ellos como lenguas de fucgo.

El trabajo de los discipulos fue noble, grande y poderoso, como el de un lider.

Las conversions comenzaron por millares. **Pero tambiern comienzan las persecucuiones**, que finalmente lograron que esas semillas se expandieran aun mas en las naciones gentiles. Una de las conversions mas importantes fue la de Saulo llamado luego Pablo, llamado el gran predicador y el **apostol** de la gente.

Pablo, transpasa fronbteras y sus viajes se propagan por Oriente y Occidente.

En la figura de Pablo encontramos la mision de Dios reflejada a su maximo esplendor.

Pablo se vale de su paciencia y humildad. Pablo cae preso por obra de los judios, Viaja a Jerusalem, Gracia, Antioquia y Roma. En Pablo vemos a un lider de las predicaciones, no muy facil de imitar.

El lider es decidido para la accion y sabe capear dificultades y como pudimos citar anteriormente el lider esta preparado para circunstancia negativas y con su valor poder afrontarlas.

Goliat en cambio confio' mas su triunfo en su fuerza que el la inteligencia.

David fue Rey y de su rama aparecen las familias de Maria y Jose.

CONCLUSIONES

Nos permitimos hacer esta conclusion, dividiendo en tres partes lo escrito en esta libro

En Primer lugar: Los lideres que tuvieron una dificil mision en interpretar a Dios en todo momento y saber escucharlo a solas o muchas veces a traves de la palabra de los profetas.

Una funcion dificil la de aquellos lideres entre los que hubo tambien Reyes, Consejos de ancianos y Jefes de Familia.

Todos los lideres en el antiguo testamento se caracterizaron por tener que llevar adelante empresas dificiles con sus pueblos.

Hemos podido ver como se producian guerras con otros pueblos y hasta luchas internas como lo pudo demostrar el pueblo elegido por Dios: Israel.

Pasando por Reyes que le dieron Paz y prosperidad a Israel y hasta otros que desoyeron la voz de Dios.

Pueblos y tribus que se descarriaron muchas veces al no querer interpretar la voz de Dios.

En los lideres mencionados en el antiguo testamente, vemos tambien el sufrimiento personal como se aprecia en Moises.

En Segundo lugar: Con la promesa de Dios se enviar un Mesias para redimir los pecados del mundo, gaciendo carne y habitando entre nosostros. Esto se aprecia en el nuevo testamento.

Lideres diferentes con un lider natural en presencia: la de Jesus.

A diferencia de los lideres en el Antiguo, ellos oian y obedecian la voluntad de Dios, aunque tenian un espiritu y caracter fuerte, fueron sumisos ante la voz de Dios.

Los lideres en el nuevo, al tener muchos de ellos la presencia del hijo, pudieron ser formados y compartir esperiencias diferentes.

Compartir la vida terrene con el hijo del creador, fue para ellos una experiencia universal totalmente fantastica.

Esos nuevos lideres formados y hechos al Mesias, lo vieron, pudieron comer con el, compartieron sus Milagros, su passion, su crucificcion y su ascension a los cielos.

Pero so decimos que los lideres en el antiguo, se diferencian sobre los del nuevo.

En tercer lugar, los lideres contemporaneos, que nos proponen la continuacion de los que abrieron el camino de la fe y de la esperanza.

Pareciera ser una tarea mas facil la de estos lideres contemporaneos pero por el contrario no lo es. En los lideres contemporaneos encontramos muchos santos y martires que aun no han sido elevados a los altares.

Hoy podemos considerar que han mas martires que en el pasado, muchos que sufren persecuciones, muchos sufren y lloran en silencio, muchos de ellos transforman su vida al no creer y perder toda esperanza.

Perdieron su fe, antes la injusticia terrena de otros hombres que alejados de Dios, cometen todo tipo de actos que denigran al ser en toda su expresion.

Tener autoridad no es lo mismo que ser autoritario decimos muchas veces. Es muy simple ver estos actos de autoritarismo en aquellos que pretendiendo ser lideres no los son.

Finalmente, podemos resumir esta conclusion, diciendo lo siguiente: Los primeros lideres oian y obedecian.

Los lideres en el nuevo testamente oian, interpretaban, compartian y discutian con su lider muchas veces.

Una etapa tal vez algom mas liberal, por compratir a diario con su lider el nuevo camino para el mundo.

En el mundo contemporaneo de hoy, los lideres continuan un camino escrito y teniendo demostraciones. Es que Dios envio' a su hijo para dar una demostracion de vida, amor y esperanza.

Los lideres contemporaneos proclaman la palabra del evangelio.

CONFESION DE
FE. ORACION DEL PECADOR

Señor Jesucristo yo se que tu fuistes crucificado en la cruz y que por tu sangre yo soy limpio de mis pecados. Ven a mi corazon te acepto como mi salvador. Porque se que al tercer dia resucitastes y estas sentado a la diestra del padre. Por tu yagas yo soy salvo de acepto Señor Jesucristo.

Si usted hiso esta oracion ya hiso su confesion de fe, le animo a que busque una biblia y asista a una iglesia local cristiana evangelica donde le enseñan como caminar y obedecer a Dios y a Jesucristo y al Espiritu Santo.